Holy Spirit

Mother

Also by Walesia Robinson Cates

My Cornerstone
compact disc of
inspirational vocal solos

Holy Spirit
Mother

...because God is family

Discover concealed Bible truths
for healing family, marriage
and gender relations

Walesia Robinson Cates, M.D.

Catesco Press

Printed in the United States of America
10 9 8 7 6 5 4 3 2 1

Attention religious organizations, women's conferences and family life conferences:
Special pricing on quantity orders for fundraisers and gifts.
Please contact the publisher:

Catesco Press
P.O Box 703
Glenn Dale Maryland 20769-2023
www.catesco.org
catescopress@catesco.org
1-800-276-8101

SAN 255-6340

Includes bibliographical references and index
ISBN: 0-9744526-0-2

Library of Congress Control Number: 2003096788

This book is printed on acid free paper.

Contents

Endorsements

"What a marvelous leap for gender studies! This profound book is a must read for all concerned with true equality between women and men. It is also a must read for those who want to realize heaven on earth. Dr. Cates is bravely walking without fearing evil. She is a precious woman."

Endesha Ida Mae Holland, Ph.D.
From the Mississippi Delta, Playwright
Professor Emeritus, The School of Theater
University of Southern California

"In an easy-to-read and timely book Dr. Cates demonstrates that the ministry of Apostle Paul reveals the expanded global impact today's Christian church will have as it embraces and utilizes the unique gifts of women in ministry and leadership. This is a must-read for anyone involved in his or her local church."

Joel A. Freeman, Ph.D.
President, The Freeman Institute

“Dr. Cates contends that God is paternal, filial, and maternal. Her book will prompt many to take a fresh look at the Trinity. The same breath of inspiration given to the German theologian Zinzendorf over 260 years ago, has also been given to Dr. Cates at the turn of the millennium.”

Barry C. Black, Ph.D., D.Min.
Chaplain, Pastor, Counselor
Washington, DC

“In her book, *Holy Spirit Mother*, Dr. Walesia Robinson Cates challenges our mind. Her approach to the Trinity is refreshing, intimidating and thought provoking. She moves outside the box and encourages us to think.”

Dr. Charles A. Ballard, Founder & CEO
“Pioneer of the Fatherhood Movement”
The Institute for Responsible Fatherhood and Family Revitalization
Headquarters, Washington, DC

"*Holy Spirit Mother* is necessary reading for women of all faiths. Even for women who study the Bible and believe they understand it, this book gives an even deeper understanding of what God intended for our families and for us.

After reading this book, we cannot help but pattern our own familial conduct after the Supreme Family of God. Thousands of years of biblical *mis*translations and *mis*interpretations have *mis*-placed us. Dr. Cates has *re*placed us to where God designed us to be.

After reading *Holy Spirit Mother*, we should never look back. God does wondrous things, and Dr. Cates leads us to understand that He indeed does many of these things through women. God bless Dr. Cates for daring to publish the dream."

The Honorable Patricia Jessamy, J.D.
Public Servant, Community Activist
Baltimore, MD

"Phenomenal! This book, *Holy Spirit Mother*, is a book every woman, and man for that matter, will love. It is filled with the anointing of the Holy Spirit, revelation knowledge and much needed instructions that will help women and men discern what is truly of God. Dr. Walesia Cates has done well in giving practical and thoughtful insights on the character, circumstances and lives of biblical women as well as women of today.

What a gift this book has given us. What a beautiful, vivid, spiritual, uplifting and encouraging picture of the lives and legacy of women who have traveled and gone on before us. I salute you, woman of God for allowing God to use you to bring healing and knowledge to hurting women all over the globe. *Holy Spirit Mother* is very timely and very much needed. Dr. Cates' personal experiences will also encourage women of all ages to strive to be all that they can be.

Schools, churches, institutions and ministries can use *Holy Spirit Mother* as a textbook, manual and reference tool for many decades to come."

Dr. Luvenia M. Miles
Counselor, Founding First Lady
International Gospel Center
Ecorse, MI

"In *Holy Spirit Mother*, Dr. Walesia Robinson Cates has opted to pursue a fresh and daring concept. She has sounded a battle cry for the consideration of what may well be a neglected aspect of femininity in the Godhead by brokering a notion and building a solid case for that notion that the presence of Father and Son figures in the Godhead necessitates a 'Mother figure' to complete the image of family. Her ideas are credible: especially so since both man and woman were created in the image and likeness of God. The book queries, 'If the idea of femininity does not inhere the Godhead, then in whose image was woman crafted?' Any serious consideration of the human family as God's basic unit would be well served by taking into account aspects of this book."

James H. Melancon
Professor Adjunct, New Testament Studies
Oakwood College
Huntsville, AL

"Sensational. What a testimony! This is an excellent resource for family devotions, Bible study and self-fulfillment."

Rev. Dr. Joseph A. Gilmore, Sr.
Pastor, Mt. Ephraim Baptist Church
Upper Marlboro, Maryland

“I can’t begin to tell you how moved and blessed I am for having read such a soul-searching book. I’ve learned so much. My husband and I had many wonderful discussions; he too has been touched. God has blessed and anointed you. As others shall read, I am sure that they will be blessed also. Congratulations!”

Ethel L. Gilmore, M.Ed.
First Lady, Mt. Ephraim Baptist Church
Upper Marlboro, Maryland

“On that sunny day of June 1977, Walesia was on a mission for the God of heaven. She introduced me to the Advent message of God’s truth. Who would have known that our encounter would lead me into the gospel ministry? And many others have been birthed into the church because of her working for and with God.

Dr. Cates’ book, *Holy Spirit Mother*, demonstrates that she is still on missions for Jehovah. This book is captivating. When you pick it up, it holds your attention and is very informative. I kept saying to myself, “I didn’t know that!” Holy Spirit Mother is a must-read for the whole family. It gives a portrait of humility, love and care for others, and a deeper knowledge of the indwelling Spirit of God. All of these are characteristics of a person in love with Christ.”

Michael Holland, M.Div.
Pastor and Counselor
Meridian, MS

Acknowledgements

Special thanks to my three little children. They make our home as heaven on earth. I thank them for their patience and understanding in allowing me time to write this book.

Thanks to Maurice Cates, my husband, for visualizing the image concept of the book's theme and creating this cover design, as well as the interior layout and formatting.

Thanks to my mother-in-law Cornelius Clay-Cates and my sister-in-law Marjorie McGann-Robinson for their attentiveness and encouragement during the finishing of this book.

Thanks to my circle of close friends that challenged me into a wider and deeper study of God's Word concerning the family unit, church history and the spirit of woman.

Thanks to my parents, Sandy and Savannah Robinson for my first experience in family.

Thanks to the women and men of various churches, groups and gatherings who have invited me, during the past two years, to share this message of the Trinity and received it with appreciation and enthusiasm.

Dedication

This book is dedicated to the person of God the Holy Spirit, third member of the Godhead. May the breath of the Spirit permeate the open window of every soul reading this book. And as God's Spirit is poured out on all flesh, may revelation knowledge be received into the good soil of each reader's heart.

I also dedicate this book to my husband, Maurice. God has joined us together, such that we are one flesh. It is because of Maurice's love and life surrounding and supporting mine, that I have confidence in the institution called family. Studying the love and life of Jesus while comparing them to those of my own husband, I can see the resemblance. As the head of His bride, the church, all that Jesus does, He does for His bride. And everything Maurice does, he does for me. He protects, empowers, pampers and provides for me. He helps me to be productive. Our unified efforts yield synergistic productivity. Maurice faithfully encouraged me through the completion of this project. What a wonderful man, my best friend and devoted companion. I love you, "Dearest." May you continue to pattern our family after the similitude of the God family, for the "kingdom of God is within you" (Luke 17:21).

Walesia, II, my daughter, is the tender person God used to plant the seed of relational hope for all humankind, in the writing of this book. It is because of her question concerning the Godhead that a place was prepared within my spirit. And God the Holy Spirit revealed Herself to me in that place. Therefore, this book is dedicated to my little girl as well, my heir, heir of God and joint-heir with Christ, an heir according to the promise. I Love you.

Foreward

I have known Walesia for over 20 years. Having observed her life since our college years together, she has exhibited a profound dedication to spirituality, both in service and lifestyle. She was fondly known on the campus as "songbird." Those melodious renditions of inspirational songs during worship services escorted us into the very presence of God. And as a serious student of science, Walesia took the time to serve the community, the church and the school. And now with the writing of this groundbreaking book she provides service in rendering historical facts, scriptural evidence and inspired exposition to the world. Combining these with familial application, she shows that each member within the earthly family unit was created to resemble and to represent the corresponding member within the heavenly family unit of God, the holy Trinity.

Whatever your theological presuppositions might be concerning the nature of God, Dr. Walesia Cates raises issues in this book that will challenge, edify, educate and expose you to a fresh dimension of His personage.

Throughout the patriarchal ages of the biblical Writes, and the subsequent millennia of male dominated Bible scholarship, whose job it was to expound upon and interpret those writings, everything about God was depicted and described in male dominated language. Most of us cannot visualize any component of the triune nature of God as anything but male. God the Father is seen as male, God the Son is seen as male, and God the Holy Spirit is seen as male.

Dr. Cates forces us to answer this question, "If man was created in the image of God, then in whose image was woman created?" The Genesis account clearly indicates that both man and woman were created in that divine image, although God is most often spoken of in masculine terms in subsequent passages. But if mankind which includes both male and female, were created in the image of God and as we say in theological terms are the *imago dei* of God, then in which part of that divine manifestation is the woman depicted. She must be depicted somewhere in the Trinity, unless we are willing to say that woman was not created in the image of God. God is the Father. Christ is the Son. What then would that make the Holy Spirit?

It would be unrealistic to expect that everyone would agree with Dr. Cates' premise and treatise. But agree or disagree, the evidence she brings to bear on the subject is overwhelmingly undeniable. Dr. Cates postulates and proves beyond a reasonable doubt, that there is significant substantiation in Scripture that the Holy Spirit is spoken of in female and motherly terms. If it is acceptable for God the Father to be spoken of in masculine and fatherly terms, and the unity of family is a reflection of the Godhead, then it is also reasonable for the Holy Spirit to be spoken of in female and motherly terms.

If you are a woman this book will educate you, inspire you, and elevate you to a new spiritual dimension. Once you pick it up you will not want to put it down. Dr. Cates will connect with you—to the core of your being. You will share in her highs and lows, her trials and her triumphs, her sacrifices and her successes, as she skillfully intertwines pieces of her life with a fresh, strong theological perspective. Her book is theological, devotional, and yet clearly practical.

If you are a man, this book will enlighten and invite you to think differently about God, about women, and about your understanding of male leadership. One must also agree that even as it is true that no man can come into the world except through the womb of his mother, even so no one can come to God except he is born through the womb of the Holy Spirit.

Errol T. Stoddart, D.Min
Pastor, New Life SDA Church
Gaithersburg, MD
Author, *The Silent Shout*

Summary

This book is for you
if you were born of a woman,
if you are a woman,
if you know a woman,
if you want to learn about woman,
if you are a mother,
if you want to be a mother,
if you know a mother,
if you want to know about mother,
if you are part of a family,
if you will be part of a family,
if you plan to make a family,
if you know a family,
if you want to know about family,
if you need a family,
if you love the concept of family,
if you respect family,
if you do not respect family,
if you need a model family,
if you desire truth of the God family.
Because Family and family,
Woman and woman,
Mother and mother
matter!

This book goes beyond religion,
beyond denomination,
beyond culture,
and
beyond tradition.

This book gets to the eternal truth that
the God family consists of
God, the heavenly Father;
God, the begotten Son;
and
God, the Holy Spirit Mother.

As you read this book,
your life will change
and change, and...
and only you
can determine the result.

“God eternal Father,
Holy Spirit Mother,
our triune connection
is Jesus, elder Brother.”

Introduction

As we are lead through the reading of this book we will see the revolutionary discovery concerning the person of the Holy Spirit, the third member of the holy Trinity. We will take a look at the roles and functions of the Spirit within the family unit called God. We will review the life of Jesus in the New Testament while observing Him as a member of the heavenly family unit and of the earthly family unit. We will see how He is indeed the *triune connection*, our connection to the heavenly God family.

Adam and Eve, as we know, were the first two members of the first earthly family. But they did not make up the very first family. There was another one called God. The God family is the original, perfect, holy family of the universe. And from this heavenly family, everything else was created. In the beginning, during the creation week, God created living creatures and plants. He made them in a way so that each could produce and reproduce its own kind. Then on the sixth day, the God family wanted to make a human creation after Its own kind. So we see in Genesis 1:27b, "male and female created he them."

I am one of five members in the family called Cates. Each of us within the family has a different personality and carries out different roles and functions. So it is in the God family. There is Father God, Son of God and Holy Spirit God. We call this family the holy Trinity or the triune God. In the divine mirror of creation, we see that members of the human family were made in the image and after the likeness of members in the God family. And as we observe the created images in that mirror, and as we look at the distinct roles and functions in which each one operates, we can then readily visualize and understand what the Originals look like and the distinct roles in which each of Them operate. Our human forms mirror the God forms. The human family was created to resemble and to imitate the heavenly family in the earth realm.

After sin entered the family, the reflection in that mirror became distorted. Humankind lost sight of godliness, its own image, its own identity, purpose and function. However, throughout the mirror-shattered existence of the family structure and damaged gender relations, the male-gender, the man, has managed to keep Father God, to a certain extent, as the model by which to pattern his own life. The male gender has kept its identity with Deity. How many sermons have we heard preachers deliver taken from the prayer Jesus prayed to His heavenly Father while here on earth? "Our Father which art in heaven, Hallowed be thy name. Thy kingdom come. Thy will be done in earth, as it is in heaven. Give us this day our daily bread. And forgive us our debts, as we forgive our debtors. And lead us not into temptation, but deliver us from evil: For thine is the kingdom, and the power, and the glory, forever. Amen" (Matthew 6:9-13). This passage of scripture has been dissected, expounded, taught and applied for many years. Those of the male gender use it to get a picture, a pattern for life as a man, husband and father. Men have been taught to recognize their identity with Father God and to celebrate it.

Just as men, husbands and fathers recognize and celebrate their heavenly model while carrying out their responsibilities and enjoying unique privileges, so should women, wives and mothers. The time has come for the truth to be unveiled. The time has come for us to discover the unchanged Word of God about the woman, her blessing, God's command for her fruitfulness and dominion, and her heavenly model.

Somewhere along the way, after sin entered the human family, only the male-man was seen as having been made in God's image. This perception has understandably lead to the belief that the Godhead consists of masculine figures only, excluding any possibility of feminine Deity.

The Son of God came to earth in the fullness of time to restore God's image on earth. And in Him "dwelleth the fulness of the Godhead bodily" (Colossians 2:9). Just as there was a Jesus-to-woman interaction at the beginning of each higher level of His ministry while here on earth, there have been women involved in the building up of His post-ascension ministry within the church. And as we stand at the door of yet a higher level of activity in the body of Christ today, I believe that we should review historical roles in which women have participated. And we are to recognize their importance, embrace and celebrate their contributions as we live in the end time, preparing for the second coming of our Lord.

Although most modern translations have changed some scriptural texts referring to God in feminine terms, we will look at some lingering clues and imageries in the original Hebrew translation. And it is from here that we can get back to the truth of the matter. We will see that indeed both male and female have representation in the God family. Jesus said to His Father, "Thy will be done on earth as it is in heaven."

After sin entered the earthly family, much went wrong in relationship between the male and female genders. After Eve and Adam individually chose to disobey God's command in the Garden of Eden, the woman's *timidity*, fearful emotions caused by sin and by Adam's accusation against her, led her to the *toleration* of Adam's attitude toward her as a woman. This toleration gave way for sinful *tradition* to take root. And sinful tradition has led to *tragedy* for the female gender and for the family structure, with global implications. Society has been built on such a tragic and faulty foundation.

The rightful place of influence, blessing, equality and dominion given to the woman by the God family has eluded her for millennia. The *reality* of sin led to the *response* in sinfulness, which led to the *result* of sinful tradition. As we know, many times in the past, the traditional beliefs of society have been in direct opposition to the truth of God.

Father God and Holy Spirit God sent forth the Son of God to give us direction and a right perspective, the heavenly view of the earthly family and of the woman. He came to reconcile the sinful family to the holy God family. He came to give back what sin has stolen. Jesus Christ came to earth, all God and all man, to show us how to live, how to think, how to relate to one another and how to have wholeness within the family unit.

Only as we accept and live the truth as it is in Christ Jesus, will we realize that each one of us—male and female alike is accepted, loved, valued, represented and celebrated in the family called God. When we accept the person and principles of Jesus we will experience the fullness of joy, the abundant life that God has made available to us, on this earth and in this lifetime. *The good news is that the family unit on earth will begin to be restored when the image of God is restored within the family unit.* We know that the basic unit in society is the family. Society simply reflects the values of the family. As we look at our society, what conclusions can we make concerning family? Where there is a missing ingredient, the "whole" does not exist. And where purpose and function are misunderstood and devalued, misuse and abuse follow. The motherly, feminine figure has been missing in our conceptualization of the Godhead. Therefore, the importance of the motherly, feminine figure within the family unit and in society has been marginalized. We can see why, then, dysfunctional family systems are prevalent globally. There is no wonder why domestic violence, rape, incest, depression, suicide, homicide, infidelity, alcoholism and many other generational iniquities plague the family unit worldwide.

This book may be used for individual Bible study, group study, church study, family ministries, women's ministries, men's ministries, singles' ministries, pre-marital counseling and for teens' ministries. I do hope that each person would posses his own copy to read and reread as often as necessary.

And because God-to-human relations, gender relations and family issues existed before there were different races of people, before there were different denominations, before there were different cultures and different socio-economic classes, this book speaks to the deepest structure of each unique condition in our human race.

This book answers two of life's three basic questions, "Who am I?" and "Why am I here?" What the reader chooses to do with these two answers will determine his/her answer to the third question of life, "Where am I going?"

One of my favorite songs speaks of peace on earth beginning with oneself. And so I believe that if families everywhere would just read this book and live out the principles to which it refers, our world would surely experience "peace and love multiplied" (Jude 2). This is my desire and prayer for all of us.

May the Spirit of the Lord illuminate your mind through the study of this revelation from God's holy Word. And as you partake of God's eternally fresh Bread, may you be satisfied!

Chapter One

Family First

The Roots

We are going to have to go back into our past, our roots, before we get into our today and our tomorrow. Let us deal with the root before we check out the shoot and the fruit. Then, as Walesia II, my 7-year-old daughter said to me one day in the year 2002, "Mother, let's change the future, today." Walesia II, the eldest of our three children, entered the library as I began writing this book. Without knowing what I was doing or writing about, she stepped into the room, saying, "Mother, let's change the future today." Then she immediately left the room.

Looking back on the sequence of events, I pinpoint July 1999 as the time I began teaching our three young children the concept of the three-in-one God. I dedicated the first week to teaching them about God, our heavenly Father. During the second week the focus was on Jesus Christ, Son of God, our elder Brother. Then at the beginning of the third week, Walesia II, then 5-years-old, said: "Mommy, I need you to teach us about God, the Mother, and God, the Daughter." Gasping for breath in search of a reply, I stumbled through some kind of superficial explanation as this seed was planted into my spirit.

I cannot remember my response to her, and we did not discuss it again until February 2002. During this time I was called to a fast through a dream, which was later confirmed by the Holy Spirit through a divine appointment. In this dream my oldest son, Maurice II, then age 5, and I were in fervent prayer. As the scene became smaller the numbers "3/40" appeared in bold red and became larger and larger until the entire view was filled with these numbers.

As this scene slowly faded, a voice said again and again: "These only come forth by fasting and prayer." I woke up in a sweat. My heart was racing. Then after confirmation, I entered a 43-day fast during which time many wonderful, supernatural events happened to me and to my family as well. During the beginning of the third week of the fast, this book that you are now reading came to me in a two-part dream. The first dream began with the words, "And so my dear sister." I felt as though the dream had lasted a very long time. When I woke up many Bible texts poured from my mouth. I felt the urgency to write down all the things I had heard in the dream. As I raced to the family library to script this dictation, something didn't feel right. Why would any writing or speech start out with the words, "And so"? These words imply that something had been said beforehand, and that was not the case. But I continued writing all I had heard.

The following night I entered into a second dream. In the morning I woke up again in a sweat, my heart racing and texts pouring from my lips. Again I rushed down to the library and wrote what I had heard. After pages and pages of short-form writing, I had finished transcribing the dictation. A voice-like impression said to me, "Now put this writing on top of the writing from yesterday. Then you will have *our* message." The seed that had been planted within my spirit two and one-half years before, by our daughter's question, had come to harvest by God's answer in two dreams.

Let us pray. *Holy triune God, Elohim, open our minds as we open Your Word. Guide us into all truth. We study. We learn. We live and we pray in the name of Jesus and to the glory of God. Amen.*

Let us explore the living Word as found in **Genesis, the New International Version:**

First: "Then God said, 'Let us make man in our image, in our likeness.' So God created man in His own image, in the image of God He created him; male and female he created them" **(1:26, 27).** It is very important to note that this word, *man*, is a word that means humankind, people, and human creatures in the Hebrew. It does not mean the male gender. The word, *man*, is the Hebrew word *'adam*, the generic name of the "human race as originally created, and afterward, like our *man*, a person, whether man or woman" (*The New Unger's Bible Dictionary.* Chicago, Ill. Moody Press: 1988, page 808). And the proper noun, *Adam*, essentially means *of the earth.* Human beings, male and female, were made from the dust of the earth.

Second: "The Lord God took the man and put him in the Garden of Eden to work it and take care of it. And the Lord commanded the man, 'You are free to eat from any tree in the garden; but you must not eat from the tree of the knowledge of good and evil, for when you eat of it you will surely die.' Then the Lord God made a woman from the rib he had taken out of the man, and He brought her to the man" **(2:15-17, 22).**

Third: "'You will not surely die,' the serpent said to the woman. When the woman saw that the fruit of the tree was good for food and pleasing to the eye, and also desirable for gaining wisdom, she took some and ate it. She also gave some to her husband, who was with her, and he ate it" **(3:4, 6).**

My version of their conversation reads something like this:

Eve: Look, Honey, I baked this delicious fruit pie for you.

Adam: M-m-m! Where did you get the fruit? It looks a little different from the fruit you usually use in pies."

Eve: Well, I got it from the *special* tree, for this *special* dinner.

Adam: You mean th-th-th-that *forbidden* tree?

Eve: Well, yes, Adam. I tasted a piece of the fruit, because the snake said it would be great.

Adam: The *snake* said?

Eve: Yes Adam, the snake said exactly that. Why do you ask?

Adam: A-h-h, Eve, snakes don't talk!

Eve: Well, all I know is that I made this fruit pie just for you. I even broke my nail trying to make it. Are you going to eat it or not?

Adam: Well, no. I-I-I can't eat *that.*

Eve: You know what Adam? It's going to be a very l-o-o-ng time before I try to do something nice for you again.

Adam: OK! OK! Give me a slice.

"Then the man and his wife heard the sound of the Lord God as he was walking in the garden in the cool of the day, and they hid from the Lord God among the trees of the garden. But the Lord God called to the man, 'Where are you?' The man said, 'The woman you put here with me—she gave me some fruit from the tree, and I ate it.' The woman said, 'The serpent deceived me, and I ate'" **(3:8-13).**

"Adam named his wife Eve, because she would become mother of all living" **(3:20).**

"So the Lord God banished him from the Garden of Eden to work the ground from which he had been taken" **(3:23).**

Fourth: "Adam lay with his wife Eve, and she became pregnant and gave birth to Cain. She said, 'With the help of the Lord I have brought forth a man'" **(4:1).**

Now let us review a few facts and questions:

The triune family of God worked together in the creation event. Man and woman were both made in the image and likeness of God. In the God family, there are three distinct personalities: Father God, Son of God, and Holy Spirit God.

God created the human male first, the man. The Hebrew word for male is *iysh.* He gave him a name, a job, a home and house-rules before He made the human female, the woman. The Hebrew word for female is *ishsah.* In working on the job that God gave the man, naming animals and keeping up his garden home, he learned a few things. One of the things he learned was that snakes don't talk.

This man also came to realize that, unlike the God family, he was alone. Someone was missing. Then, using the man's rib, God made the woman, completing the work He had already planned.

Before long the couple ventured into the central area of the garden. The man was with the woman at this time or perhaps joined her later at the forbidden tree. This couple gives us a great example of being a hearer of the Word but not a doer of the Word. Both of them had heard the words of God concerning what to eat and what not to eat. And since both of them, Adam and Eve, had perfect memories at that time, the spoken Word was all they needed. The Bible says, "I have set before you life and death, blessing and cursing: therefore choose life" (Deuteronomy 30:19). The woman, Eve, by being deceived in a conversation with Satan, chose death. She was to blame for her own choice to sin. The man, Adam, not having been deceived, willfully chose to disobey God, and was responsible for his own choice as well.

Here are some questions that I have asked myself about Adam and Eve's experience:

- If the woman, Eve, was not in Adam's presence when she went to the central area of the garden, did he know where she was?
- If he knew she wasn't with him, why didn't he call out for her or go to look for her?
- Did he care that she was alone and therefore exposed to possibly meeting up with Lucifer, the fallen one?
- If he did not know she had left his side, why not? Was he paying more attention to his work than to his wife?
- Had Adam taken the time to go over a family mission statement and the house rules with Eve, as God had done with him before the woman was made? If he did, was he sure that his wife understood everything the way that he understood?

For those who believe that Adam was right there with Eve at the forbidden tree, I ask more questions:

- Why did Adam allow the serpent and the woman to have the conversation in the first place? Why did he not step in to protect his wife from such trickery? He knew more about the animals than she did. Why wasn't he on the J-O-B protecting his family like a husband should? Why did he keep silent during this critical conversation? Does this mean he wanted to eat it too?
- And as an aside, when God looked over His work of creation, He said that it was good. God gave credit to Himself for what He made because that is where the credit belongs. When He created woman to complete the family made in His image and likeness and presented her to Adam, why didn't Adam give the credit to God for what He had made? I have not seen any texts implying his verbal gratitude to the Creator for a help meet that "was not found" earlier (Genesis 2:18). Adam congratulated himself with, "This is bone of *my* bone and flesh of *my* flesh" (verse 23). Why? Adam was very quick to speak out at this magnificent creation moment. So why did he not speak out when this same woman was being tricked at the forbidden tree? Was his initial and basic approach to the woman, and to the family unit, bending in the direction that would eventually end in tragedy?

On the other hand, perhaps Adam was simply saying that since the female-man, taken from the rib of the male-man and was formed by God in the same manner as he had been, then the two of them are of the same essence and are equal, with different characteristics, in order to completely reflect the image of God. Therefore the male-man gave God's newest creation, his female counterpart, the name "woman," which basically means *man with a womb.* Male and female were the names God gave them respectively. He also called them "man." Adam-male-man in his perfection said that the female-man could also be called "woman," as the counterpart to male-man. And God already used the word *woman* before Adam did (Genesis 2:22). We will take a deeper look at the name "Eve" in chapter three. But for now, let's just call the female-man, the woman, by the name, Eve. And we will refer to the male-man as Adam.

And so, what about the woman?

- Did Eve see herself as a woman of leisure and as God's gift to man? Did she think that gardening and caring for the animals were beneath her or that these were a man's job?
- Did she exert a natural influence on Adam and tell him to just keep on working because she had somewhere to go and would be right back?
- Did she tell Adam not to follow her around because she was grown and just as independent as he?
- Did she convince him to just do his own thing and let her do her own thing? Did she not realize that Adam had been around longer than she had, and just might know some things she didn't know?
- Did she think she could handle the devil alone, because she too was made in God's image and likeness?

And, finally, what about the couple?

- If Adam was by her side at the tree, as some say he was, why did she not prompt Adam to speak up? Why did she make this important decision without her husband's input? Why did she not suggest that they talk it over and come to a mutual agreement?

- Did Adam and Eve not think it important to follow the example of the perfect triune family of God, of being separate individuals yet unified in purpose and activity? Or did they want to try a new way?
- Why is the first recording of the couple's coming together, as husband and wife, not until after they were put out of the Garden of Eden? Just stop and think about this garden that God had given to them. What a wonderful setting for loving: a beautiful floral atmosphere; lush, green, soft carpet-grass; canopies of low tree branches wrapped with grape vines. Large, sweet, juicy berries and fruit were just within arm's reach. There were sounds of happy birds and flowing streams, soft flutters of butterflies and gentle morning breezes. They even had moonlit nights with dreamy silhouettes. What a set up. God is L-O-V-E. Why would they wait for eviction from their beautiful garden home to experience the highest human pleasure on barren, dusty, thorny, cursed grounds? What a waste.

Are there messages and lessons in this tragedy for us today? God told them that if they ate of the forbidden tree, they would surely die. And that is exactly what happened instantly:

- Their innocence died.
- Their closeness as companions died.
- Their mutual trust died.
- The shining glory surrounding them died.
- The appreciation for their beautiful bodies that had been sculpted by God Himself, died.

- Their ability to walk with God in the cool of the day died.
- Their understanding of equality within the family structure died.

Sin did a job on them. God told them what would happen if they disobeyed, and yet they still disobeyed. This perfect couple literally hand made and match made by God became dysfunctional when they went against the will of God. Inequality within the family structure as a result of sin has resulted in pain, hate, brutality, domestic violence, suspicion, jealousy, rage, infidelity, injustice, and much more. All of this is outside the will of God for humankind.

God knows everything. He knows what is best for us. Don't try to figure out why He is saying what He is saying. Don't try to come up with the how, the when, the why, and the where about this or that. Don't talk to snakes about what God said, because snakes don't really talk.

God is smarter than we are. God has more information than we have. God can see farther than we can see. God can think clearer than we can think. God knows everything about everything—all the time.

"For my thoughts are not your thoughts, neither are your ways my ways, saith the Lord. For as the heavens are higher than the earth, so are my ways higher than your ways, and my thoughts than your thoughts" (Isaiah 55:8, 9).

Just trust God and obey Him. It's the best way to live. And it is the only way to live well. "For the wages of sin is death; but the gift of God is eternal life through Jesus Christ our Lord" (Romans 6:23). "Justice and judgment are the habitation of thy throne: mercy and truth shall go before thy face" (Psalms 89:14). "Mercy and truth are met together; righteousness and peace have kissed each other" (Psalms 85:10).

Justice demanded punishment for sin, but mercy demanded forgiveness of sin. The triune family of God is merciful, longsuffering, just, gracious and abundant in goodness and compassion toward us. The contingency plan of redemption was set into motion. "For God sent not His Son into the world to condemn the world; but that the world through him might be saved" (John 3:17). "He [God] sent his word, and healed them, and delivered them from their destructions" (Psalms 107:20).

Chapter Two

FAMILY to Family

And now, let us fast forward to the New Testament.

John 1: 10-14, NIV. "He was in the world, and though the world was made through him, the world did not recognize him. He came to that which was his own, but his own did not receive him. Yet to all who received him, to those who believed in his name, he gave the right to become children of God—children born not of natural descent, nor of human decision or a husband's will, but born of God. The Word became flesh and made his dwelling among us. We have seen his glory, the glory of the One and Only, who came from the Father, full of grace and truth."

Matthew 1: 18-25, NIV. "This is how the birth of Jesus Christ came about: His mother Mary was pledged to be married to Joseph, but before they came together, she was found to be with child through the Holy Spirit. Because Joseph her husband was a righteous man and did not want to expose her to public disgrace, he had in mind to divorce her quietly. But after he had considered this, an angel of the Lord appeared to him in a dream and said, 'Joseph son of David, do not be afraid to take Mary home as your wife, because what is conceived in her is from the Holy Spirit. She will give birth to a son, and you are to give him the name Jesus, because he will save his people from their sins.' All this took place to fulfill what the Lord had said through the prophet: 'The virgin will be with child and will give birth to a son, and they will call him Immanuel'—which means, 'God with us.' When Joseph woke up, he did what the angel of the Lord had commanded him and took Mary home as his wife…she gave birth to a son. And he gave him the name Jesus."

Good Company; Pure Lineage

So Jesus Christ came to this earth to go through all that fallen human beings go through. He put on an earth suit, human flesh. He laid aside His divinity. He handicapped himself with humanity. He became susceptible to pain, disappointment, discouragement, hunger, thirst, loneliness, and grief. He did all this so that He could understand, sympathize, and empathize with us. He knows what we know and feels what we feel. Jesus was tempted in all points as we are, yet without sin (Hebrews 4:15). He was acquainted with *grief*—not just sporadic disappointments and tough Monday mornings.

Grief, according to *Webster's Unabridged Dictionary,* means "keen mental suffering or distress over affliction or loss; sharp sorrow." So He felt what we have felt.

Jesus came to earth to get the victory, to get the authority over sin and over the works of darkness. And He came to pay the wages of sin for us: death. He came to bring the human race back into right relation with God. He achieved these goals through His birth, life, death, resurrection, ascension and high priestly ministry.

Christ Jesus was born in a stable. He was born with a price on his little head. Herod was waiting for him, holding a sword behind his back. And let me add here, that Herod represents the dragon,

Satan, in the book of Revelation. Herod also represents any institution in the church or in society that oppresses or puts down any race, gender, socioeconomic class, or sub-group of these entities.

The Wise Men who were commissioned by King Herod to bring back a report of the Christ-child's location proved to be wise indeed. They were instrumental in the child's escape to safety. Jesus was a refugee in a foreign land during his infancy. Then He finally made it home, the city of Nazareth. Jesus grew up in the slums of Nazareth, learned of and endured the raw culture of debased human experience day in and day out for 30 years. This slum city was so infamous that Jesus' very authenticity was questioned: "Can there any good thing come out of Nazareth?" (John 1:46).

During this time in history women were considered as mere property. They were considered backseat, second-class, sideline dwellers with all that this would imply in the economic structure, in the church, in the family, and in society as a whole. Jesus saw the actions against and the attitudes toward women. He saw women accepting the hand that was dealt to them. So He certainly could have simply accepted that prevailing way of life. But I believe that having been raised in a home handpicked by the God family, Jesus grew up experiencing mutual respect by and for all family members. This was the structure He had ordained in the very beginning, as Creator of this world. So we find in the Bible that Jesus' incarnation is an invitation to liberty, an invitation to life abundant, an invitation to openness, and an invitation to salvation from oppression.

In this Jewish economy, males protected their bloodline. There was a waiting period between the time a couple was engaged to the actual time that they were married. During the waiting season, about six months, it would become apparent if the bride-to-be was pregnant. If the she were found to be with child, wedding plans would come to a screeching halt. Since there was not an accurate, objective, analytical way of knowing the identity of the unborn child's father, the groom would give her a bill of divorce in a public setting and hand her back to her father. This was the softer alternative to having her put to death.

Such was the predicament in which Mary and Joseph found themselves. The Bible says that Joseph was a just man, fair and upright, a good-hearted gentleman who had good motives. In other words, he was a righteous man. Yes, he was far ahead of his time. Righteous people seem to be ahead of their time. He obviously did not sanction public humiliation of women, because he tried to figure out a way to save Mary from this ordeal and yet get her back to her father's house.

After Joseph had settled in his mind to do this gentlemanly act, the angel of the Lord appeared to him and told him exactly what to do (Matthew 1: 18-25). He said to him, in so many words: Joseph, do not be afraid to take Mary home as your wife. The baby that she is carrying is not another man's child. Don't worry. You will not have to support another man's bloodline. In fact, this child comes from Yahweh. People are going to call him Immanuel, God with us. I want you to put on his birth certificate the name Jesus. He is here to save his people from their sins. You see, Joseph, this child has nothing to do with the Jewish economy. All the silver, the gold, the gems of the earth, the mountains and hills, and the cattle on those hills over there already belong to this Son of God. Your bloodline is safe with him. His economy is of a spiritual nature. And this child will become *your* ticket out of this world into paradise. So don't worry, Joseph. Everything is going to be all right.

Virtuous Qualities

I believe that one of the reasons God chose Mary to be the mother and the steward of His Son was because of the person to whom she was engaged, the company she kept. She was judged and chosen on the basis of her choice of companionship. If Joseph were not a just man; if he thought like the other men and went along with the system's traditional treatment of women; if he had favored condemnation of women; if he had been interested in flexing and showing that he was boss at all cost; had he been disposed to meting out public humiliation or even private humiliation of women, God would not have chosen Mary because of the company she kept. When dealing in human affairs, in humanity's sinful state, God does not manipulate persons to get the job done. He chooses those whom He can use for His purposes.

Joseph saw in Mary the same virtuous qualities that Father God saw in Mary. They both chose her. The average man in that day and culture would have done the average thing: Dragged Mary out to the church elders and city fathers and publicly shoved her back to her father, or worse.

If Joseph had given Mary a bill of divorce, then Mary's child would not have been authenticated as the incarnate Son of God. The take-home lesson here, friends, is watch the company you keep.

Your seed of divine destiny will never be realized while hanging around the wrong folks. Your anointing, your prosperity, your predestined place in God's eternal plan will never come to fruition in the wrong company.

Where there is an attitude of superiority, God will not manifest in His fullness. Where there is contempt for diversity, God will not work in His fullness. Where there is an attitude of unfairness, polarity, and inequity, God will not reside.

Your seed of divine destiny will never be realized while hanging around the wrong folks. Your anointing, your prosperity, your predestined place in God's eternal plan will never come to fruition in the wrong company.

Where there is a lifestyle of impurity, unthankfulness, ungodliness, laziness, strife, unforgiveness, and selfishness, God will not be in it.

Joseph, being obedient to the voice of God, took Mary home in marriage. He was led step by step in caring for his adopted son. What a man! It will be good to see him in heaven someday and watch him interact with the heavenly family of God!

And now let us turn our attention to Mary. Calculated to have been between the ages of 14 and 17, Mary was blessed above all women to be chosen by God. It is very interesting to see that after Mary's encounter with the angel, this teenager revealed an attitude of submission. How common is that?

In her acceptance response, off the top of her head, she quoted 15 different scriptural passages in praise to God. This tells me that she was a young woman of the Word. She was a worshipper. It's no wonder that she was the chosen one. This young lady was already in a relationship with God. They were friends, with a Spirit-to-spirit connection. So the Spirit-to-spirit connection led to a Family-to-family connection. She already knew God and His voice. She already understood that He works by supernatural means for the natural. She had already developed the faith to know that what God says He will do, is already done. What a wonderful young lady! Mary's first words about what was to come forth from her were of submission to God, consent to God, and praise to God—not praise of herself. What a contrast to Adam's words after Eve was brought forth from him. So the couple, Mary and Joseph, was a match made in heaven. Here are two people whom God could count on.

Speaking of Spirit-to-spirit connection, when you walk by faith you are in a spirit-connected mode. You are in fellowship and communion with God. This is true worship. In this type of connection God will reveal His mysteries and deposit His own thoughts about you into your spirit. He will tell you what He is doing in your life before He allows it to manifest. So it won't matter how things appear to your eyes, you are going by what God told you. You will walk by faith and not by sight.

Where there is an attitude of superiority, God will not manifest in His fullness. Where there is contempt for diversity, God will not work in His fullness. Where there is an attitude of unfairness, polarity, and inequity, God will not reside.

Despite what your situation and circumstances look like in the natural, you already know the outcome. This is how you can have peace in the midst of a storm! You will not react to your situation; you will react to your revelation! You will not react to your circumstance; you will react by your spirit-stance.

So you can rejoice in the fact that the storm is passing over. Hallelujah! It is your spirit that seeks after God, not your flesh. So worship Him in spirit and in truth. The Bible says that when you search for Him with all of your heart, you will find Him.

Chapter Three

Family Spirit

Speaking of the Spirit, let us turn our attention to the heavenly family unit, the three-in-one God. This means three persons or personalities united in one family unit. We call this God family unit, the holy Trinity, the holy Triune or the Godhead. The triune family consists of Father God, Son of God, and Holy Spirit God, as explained in the holy Word of God. Let us take a look at 1 John 5:7, "For there are three that bear record in heaven, the Father, the Word, and the Holy Ghost; and these three are one." Then in John 10:30 we find that Jesus says, "I and my Father are one." A Hebrew name for God, Elohim, literally means, "The Gods." In the Hebrew, The "***El***" of Elohim is the masculine God, the "***him***" is the feminine God." I am aware that some say human beings should not try to comprehend the Trinity through anthropomorphic conceptualization. However, the Bible has already given us permission to do so. And it even gives us the window through which we are to look for such understanding. With our human minds, the only way we can understand the Godhead is through such conceptualization. This is especially true in the light of our being created in God's image. We are to understand God the way He has revealed Himself.

Throughout the Bible we read of God referring to His body parts, feelings, thoughts and plans. God speaks to us human beings in the way we can indeed understand. Throughout the Bible we see plural personal pronouns in reference to the Trinity. But we also see each member of the Trinity as an individual personality. When creating humankind, God uses the plural pronouns of *us* and *our*, in Genesis 1:26, in reference to the Trinity. And in creating humankind in Their image, we see that the Hebrew word used for image is *tselem,* meaning resemblance and outward appearance. And we know that this word is used in reference to outward appearance, because it is also used in other scriptures, such as Genesis 5:1-3; 9:6; Exodus 20:4; Psalms 73:20 and others, when speaking of physical appearance. And the Hebrew word for likeness is *demuwth*, meaning model, similitude, shape and resemblance (Dake Annotated Reference Bible, page 618). In Genesis 3:22, God again uses, in reference to Himself, plural pronouns, when He says the phrase, "*as one of us*."

I am one of five persons in the Cates family. We are one family. Yet each of us is an individual, a unique personality with different responsibilities, and different family roles. And so it is in the family called God. There are three distinct personalities who have different responsibilities and roles. Each is God. And each shares the essence of deity. Jesus Christ, the Son of God, prayed to Father God while here on earth, "Thy will be done on earth, as it is in heaven" (Matthew 6:10).

Within the structure of the holy Trinity family, we are going to look for scriptural revelation about the personality of God, the Holy Spirit. Then we will get to the conclusion about the Holy Spirit's person and ministry as they relate to the woman.

Let us start with this poem I wrote when teaching my children about the Holy Spirit:

Sweet, sweet Holy Spirit,
I invite your presence here today.
Anoint my eyes that I may see
the love and care
You give to me.
Anoint my ears that I may hear
That still, small voice
speak words of cheer.
Anoint my hands that I may reach
to share your blessings
and Your gospel teach.
Anoint my feet that I may run
To tell the world
that Jesus will come.
Anoint my life and through me show
Your love to others
So they too will know.
I thank You for anointing me.
In Jesus name, Amen.

This is what the Word of the Lord says:

Genesis 1:1, 2: "In the beginning God created the heaven and the earth. And the earth was without form, and void; and darkness was upon the face of the deep. And the Spirit of God moved upon the face of the waters. And God said, 'Let there be light.' And there was light."

Move is the same as the Hebrew *hover.* It means protecting and participating in creative work as a feminine activity. The Holy Spirit saw darkness and disorder in the earth and "moved" or "hovered," initiating creative change. By far the wife and mother, the woman in a family home initiates and carries out the cleaning and organizing of the house. She recruits assistance from the family members. So after the Holy Spirit moved upon the face of the deep in order to initiate creative change and to restore order, then the fertile word of Father God came forth, "Let there be light: and there was light" (Genesis 1:3). The meaning of *hover* is found in another passage of Scripture, Deuteronomy 32:11. There it refers to an eagle hovering to protect her hatchlings. The Word of Father God is God's Son. And the Son is the "express image of his person [the Father]" (Hebrews 1:3). The Bible says, "God's *Word* became flesh and dwelt among us" (John 1:14). As in a good family, the children carry out the will of the father and mother. The Bible says "By the *word* of the Lord were the heavens made; and all the host of them by the breath of his mouth. For he *spake*, and it was done; he *commanded,* and it stood fast" (Psalms 33:6, 9).

Holy Spirit Mother, Father God, and Son of God worked together in creation. It was a family affair. The Holy Spirit was the initiator and creative force in the "birthing" of the earth and its inhabitants. *Earth* in the original Hebrew translation is referred to as "she," according to *The Interlinear NIV Hebrew-English Old Testament* Bible. Because the She God initiated the creative project, the earth that She created was given a feminine name. This is why we call nature by the name "Mother Nature." We also call lands of the earth the "Mother Land."

"Thou sendest forth thy Spirit, they are created: and thou renewest the face of the earth" (Ps. 104:30). "By his Spirit he hath garnished the heavens; his hand hath formed the crooked serpent"

(Job 26:13). The Holy Spirit adorned the heavens at creation, and renewed the earth that was dark and without form. So we see the Spirit of God as a decorator as well.

"To appoint unto them that mourn in Zion, to give unto them beauty for ashes, the oil of joy for mourning, the garment of praise for the spirit of heaviness; that they might be called trees of righteousness, the planting of the Lord, that he might be glorified. I will greatly rejoice in the Lord, my soul shall be joyful in my God; for he hath clothed me with the garments of salvation, he hath covered me with the robe of righteousness, as a bridegroom decketh himself with ornaments, and as a bride adorneth herself with her jewels" (Isaiah 61:3, 10).

These texts speak of the Holy Spirit adorning and beautifying God's people with the robe of righteousness, bringing beauty for ashes and garments of praise to replace the spirit of heaviness. The work of adorning, beautifying, and bringing garments, like that of a seamstress, is often a womanly role.

"And I saw a new heaven and a new earth; for the first heaven and the first earth were passed away; and there was no more sea. And I John saw the holy city, new Jerusalem, coming down from God out of heaven, prepared as a bride adorned for her husband. And he carried me away in the spirit to a great and high mountain, and showed me that great city, the holy Jerusalem, descending out of heaven from God" (Revelation 21:1, 2, 10).

We can see that the Bible ends with the adorning work of the Holy Spirit in which New Jerusalem descends as a bride adorned for her husband. The Holy Spirit shows God's people the beauty of the Holy City that was prepared for them. This is just like a woman showing her guests the rooms that she prepared for their comfortable stay or showing her children their newly decorated rooms.

"As an eagle stirreth up her nest, fluttereth over her young, spreadeth abroad her wings, taketh them, beareth them on her wings" (Deuteronomy 32:11).

So in speaking of God taking care of His children, the same Hebrew word for *hover* is used to show what the eagle does over her nest of young in taking care of them, the way mothers do. It is the same meaning for *moved* as used in Genesis 1: 2 in speaking of the Holy Spirit's work, or role, or responsibility during Her creative birthing of the earth. This word signifies feminine activity.

"The Lord shall go forth as a mighty man, he shall stir up jealousy like a man of war: he shall cry, yea, roar; he shall prevail against his enemies. I have long time holden my peace; I have been still, and refrained myself; now will I cry like a travailing woman; I will destroy and devour at once. And I will bring the blind by a way that they knew not; I will lead them in paths that they have not known: I will make darkness light before them, and crooked things straight. These things will I do unto them, and not forsake them" **(Isaiah 42:13-16).**

Verse 13: God is revealed in the light of masculinity, a mighty man of war, triumphant over His enemies. God the Father would fit this description.

Verses 14-16: God is seen in the analogy of a pregnant woman whose water has broken, putting her into the pains of labor and delivery. Only a woman can do this, of course.

Verse 16: We see that God is mothering Her newborn babies.

Prophetically this is saying that the silence will be broken and the darkness of ignorance will be replaced with the light of knowledge and understanding. This is that time, I believe. The time has come for humankind to understand the God family, in image and likeness, as we should have from the beginning. Somewhere after sin entered the first family this truth was perverted, covered, lost and forgotten. Our blinded eyes will see the truth of the God family.

"And the Spirit of the Lord shall rest upon him, the spirit of wisdom and understanding, the spirit of counsel and might, the spirit of knowledge and of the fear of the Lord" (Isaiah 11:2). The Bible reveals the levels of care that the Holy Spirit gives: wisdom, understanding, counsel, power, knowledge, reverence for the Lord and comfort. This is the work of a good mother for her children. And it reminds us of the truths found in Proverbs chapters 2 and 4.

Proverbs 1:7-9 "The fear of the Lord is the beginning of knowledge; but fools despise wisdom and instruction. My son, hear the instruction of thy father, and forsake not the law of thy mother. For they shall be an ornament of grace unto thy head, and chains about thy neck." Additionally, Proverbs 1:8 reveals that both the father and the mother teach their son in the way of life. So throughout the book of Proverbs, the father is giving instruction, and the mother is giving wisdom, knowledge, and understanding to their child. The wisest man that ever lived understood the source of his giftedness. This is exactly why the writer calls wisdom "she" and dedicates the entire chapter to the Spirit of Wisdom, the Holy Spirit as the spirit of woman.

Proverbs 3:13-20 "Happy is the man that findeth wisdom, and the man that getteth understanding. For the merchandise of it is better than the merchandise of silver, and the gain therof than fine gold. She is more precious than rubies [like the virtuous woman in Prov. 31:10]; and all the things thou canst desire are not to be compared unto her. Length of days is in her right hand; and in her left hand riches and honor. Her ways are ways of pleasantness, and all her paths are peace. She is a tree of life to them that lay hold upon her; and happy is everyone that retaineth her. Then we read in verse 20, "The Lord by wisdom hath founded the earth; by understanding hath he established the heavens. By His knowledge the depths are broken up, and the clouds drop down the dew."

In these passages one can readily see that the characteristics of the Holy Spirit and references to the work and person of the Spirit are mentioned. In the first chapter the son is admonished to listen to the father's instruction and to the mother's law. So both parents are mentioned here. Then in Proverbs 3:12 the author picks up on the father's correction, but then shifts back to the mother's law of wisdom and understanding. Verse 15 calls this wisdom "she," because it is from the mother. This wisdom is "more precious than rubies" just as is the wife and mother of the family written of in Proverbs 31.

Then in Proverbs 3:18, the Spirit of wisdom, the Holy Spirit, the spirit of woman is depicted as a "tree of life" which would explain the concept of the "fruit of the Spirit." The fruit of the Spirit are from the Holy Spirit, Her ministry, Her characteristics as found in Galatians 5:22. In Proverbs 3:19 we see wisdom depicted as that which created the heavens and the earth. Verse 20 speaks on the breaking up of the depths [waters], the way that the "Spirit of the Lord moved upon the face of the deep [waters]." These verses are indeed referring to the creation story, in which we know that the Holy Spirit was the active personality. You may wish to review Genesis 1:1, 2 and compare them again with these texts. The tree of life also seen in Revelation 22:2 is referred to as "she."

Right Hand, Arm, Hand

The "right hand" and "arm" and "hand" of God in the Old Testament all represent and refer to the Holy Spirit. "O sing unto the Lord a new song; for he hath done marvelous things; his right hand, and his holy arm, that gotten him the victory. The Lord hath made known his salvation: his righteousness hath he openly showed in the sight of the heathen" (Psalms 98:1, 2).

In these passages the Holy Spirit is revealed as the Spirit of miracle-working power, Spirit of truth, and of salvation in rebirth. These are represented by the activities that Jesus did through the power of the Holy Spirit immediately after His wilderness experience (Luke 4:14, 18). And the phrase: "His holy arm, that gotten him the victory" reflects the passage found in Isaiah 59:19, "…the Spirit of the Lord will lift up a standard (victory banner) against him (the enemy)." Right hand and right arm are symbols of power.

Isaiah 30:30: "And the Lord shall cause his glorious voice to be heard, and shall show the lighting down of his arm, with the indignation of anger, and with the flame of a devouring fire, with scattering, and tempest, and hailstones."

God's voice is heard from heaven, just as it was at Jesus' baptism. And the viewers there see His Arm coming down from heaven. At Jesus' baptism the Holy Spirit came down in the form of a dove, and led him into the wilderness to receive power to devour the enemy's kingdom. At Pentecost, the power of the Holy Spirit came down as tongues of fire to devour the works of darkness. So these same New Testament events were the fulfillment of the prophetic writings in Isaiah, concerning the Holy Spirit.

Isaiah 40:10, 11: "Behold, the Lord God will come with strong hand, and his arm shall rule for him; behold his reward is with him, and his work before him. He shall feed his flock like a shepherd: he shall gather the lambs with his arm, and carry them in his bosom, and shall gently lead those that are with young." Here the Bible speaks of the Sovereign Lord's Arm ruling for Him, which is the Holy Spirit of God. And the Spirit also tends God's flock like a shepherd, carries the sheep close to God's heart, like a mother's bosom, and gently leads those with babies and young children.

And continuing with verse 12: "Who hath measured the waters in the hollow of his hand and meted out heaven with the span, and comprehended the dust of the earth in a measure, and weighed the mountains in scales, and the hills in a balance?" This text refers to the creation event, in which the Holy Spirit was the initiating force.

Isaiah 40:13, 14: "Who hath directed the Spirit of the Lord, or being his counselor hath taught him? With whom took he counsel and who instructed him, and taught him in the path of judgment, and taught him knowledge, and shewed to him the way of understanding?" So here the Bible speaks of the Spirit of wisdom, knowledge and understanding, which we know is the Holy Spirit. And as we have seen, the Spirit of wisdom is depicted as "she" in Proverbs.

Psalms 139: 10: "Your right hand (Holy Spirit) shall hold me." The Bible uses "hand of God," as one of the most comforting symbols of the Holy Spirit. The mother's gentle touch and guiding hand are what her children love and trust. And Jesus calls the Holy Spirit the Comforter (John 14:26). God is also described as a mother comforting her children, in Isaiah 66:13 and 14. It reads, "As one whom his mother comforteth, so will I comfort you; and ye shall be comforted in Jerusalem. And when ye see this, your heart shall rejoice, and your bones shall flourish like an herb: and *the hand of the Lord* shall be known toward his servants, and his indignation toward his enemies."

Both Mom and Dad

Psalms 139:7-13: "Whither shall I go from thy Spirit? Or whither shall I flee from thy presence? If I ascend up into heaven, thou art there; if I make my bed in hell, behold, thou art there. If I take the wings of the morning, and dwell in the uttermost parts of the sea; even there shall thy *hand* lead me, and thy *right hand* shall hold me. If I say, 'Surely the darkness shall cover me'; even the night shall be light about me. Yea, the darkness hideth not from thee; but the night shineth as the day: the darkness and the light are both alike to thee…thou hast covered me in my mother's womb."

This is just like a mother who watches her children, following them around and caring for them. She will go anywhere to retrieve her child. This is what the Bible says of the Holy Spirit.

John 14: 26, NKJV. "But the Helper, the Holy Spirit, whom the Father will send in my name, will teach you all things, and bring to your remembrance all things that I said to you."

Jesus, the Son of God, said that Father God would send the Helper. This "Helper" resembles the term "help meet" found in Genesis when God created the woman from the rib of the man. "Help meet" means counterpart not assistant, not servant, not slave, but complement, or member of the whole unit. The unit is not complete until all parts are present or represented.

Romans 8:15, 16. "For ye have not received the spirit of bondage again to fear; but ye have received the Spirit of adoption, whereby we cry, 'Abba, Father.' The Spirit itself beareth witness with our spirit, that we are the children of God."

So because of the Spirit of God recreating, nurturing, and developing us when we receive Christ, we cry *Abba* which means father, "a Chaldee word corresponding to the Hebrew *ab*, father" (Holman Bible Dictionary and Concordance, page 2). The Holy Spirit testifies that you are God's child. "Children" in verse 16 means "born ones," as we are born not of flesh, but of the Spirit. So the Holy Spirit is the source of our spiritual rebirth and develops us into spiritual maturity. The Holy Spirit tells us who our heavenly Father is. This is what mothers do. Children know who their father is because the mother teaches this to them, and she also teaches them to say, "Daddy" and "Father" (like "Abba").

Heavenly Model

We also know that foundational earthly systems originate in heaven, in the spirit realm. This is true of the creation week, the Sabbath, the marriage institution, and the tabernacle. For example, the tabernacle system that God gave to Moses for His people was an earthly replica of the one that God has in heaven. God gave Moses complete and detailed instructions, so that it would reflect and resemble the one in heaven. "Thy will be done on earth, as it is in heaven."

Hebrews 8 records: "A minister of the sanctuary, and of the true tabernacle, which the Lord pitched, and not man" (verse 2). "Who serve unto the temple and shadow of heavenly things, as Moses was admonished of God when he was about to make the tabernacle: for, See, saith he, that thou make all things according to the pattern shewed to thee in the mount" (verse 5). Chapter 9 adds: "It was therefore necessary that the patterns of the things in the heavens should be purified with these; but the heavenly things themselves with better sacrifices than these" (verse 23).

And to add to this, we know that at the end of the creation week Father God looked over the "work of His hands," the work of the Holy Spirit, and saw that it was very good. Then He sanctified the seventh day and rested.

According to ancient custom, the Jewish family begins the seventh day, Sabbath, at sunset Friday. The family gathers for praise and worship, prayer and blessings. The husband begins this service by praising his wife. He tells her what a good wife and mother she is, finds many things on which to compliment her and blesses her and the works of her hands. Afterwards, he pronounces blessing on each child. This is yet another shadow of what went on in heaven after the Holy Spirit completed Her creative handiwork. The custom beginning with the Ancient of Days (God) continues today within the family unit of the enlightened.

So when Jesus prayed, "Thy will be done on earth, as it is in heaven," He was referring to the role and function of the heavenly Father, just as the earthly father has for his own family. His prayer, as recorded in Matthew 6: 9-13, is essentially a model from which earthly fathers are to pattern their role within the family unit. I have paraphrased this passage of Scripture, and our children recite it for their father on Father's Day.

Tribute for Dad

Our Father, who art here with us, blessed is your name.
Your time has come.
Your will be done in our home,
For this is heaven on earth.
You provide for us daily.
Your overlooking our faults teaches us to do the same for others.
You are our spiritual guide against worldly distractions.
And you protect us from harm.
This home is yours.
You are responsible for it.
And as you abide humbly herein,
You are so worthy of respect and praise.
And to this tribute
Your children shall say,
Amen and Amen again!

Chapter Four

Family Revealed

Let us continue our discovery of the works and ways of the Holy Spirit.

Galatians 5:22, 23: "But the fruit of the Spirit is love, joy, peace, faithfulness, kindness, longsuffering, goodness, gentleness, self-control, faith, meekness, temperance; against such there is no law. If we live in the Spirit, let us also walk in the Spirit."

These are the attributes of children born of the Holy Spirit, the fruit of Her womb. In John 3:5, Jesus said to Nicodemus and to us today, "You must be born again," that is, born of the Holy Spirit. You can enjoy reading John 3:5-7 for yourself.

You can be born twice. The first time, you were born of a woman, your earthly mother. The second time you must be born of your heavenly Mother, the Holy Spirit, the help-meet of Father God, His counterpart within the holy triune family, called God. Concerning our rebirth, those who believe and receive Jesus as Messiah, the One sent of God to redeem the fallen human race from the death of sin, through the work of Holy Spirit Mother, become sons and daughters of God. We receive adoption into the heavenly, eternal family of God. Romans 8:1-17 gives the details of the rebirth process. Please take this time to read these texts.

Because of the work of Holy Spirit Mother, we too can call Father God, "Abba" as we now take our place in the heavenly family unit. Jesus becomes our elder Brother. We have obtained "the Spirit of adoption," Holy Spirit Mother. "The Spirit itself beareth witness with our spirit, that we are the children of God: And if children, then heirs; heirs of God, and joint-heirs with Christ" (verses 16 and 17). As children of God, we grow to resemble Him in character. We take on the attributes of the Holy Spirit. We reflect God.

Human beings are born of the flesh first. This is the natural birth. And as we found in the book of Genesis, all living things produce "after their kind." This is especially true in the spiritual world. As we read throughout New Testament writings, the "flesh" and the "Spirit" define opposite planes of existence. Romans 6:12-18 explains this. The natural birth and life in the flesh lead to death. But the supernatural birth and life in the Spirit lead to eternal life through Jesus Christ. Then in Galatians 5:17 Paul says, "For the flesh lusteth against the Spirit, and the Spirit against the flesh: and these are contrary the one to the other." Jesus shares humanity with our earthly family and shares divinity with our heavenly family. And through His life, death, resurrection and ministry, the two families are united again.

In Colossians 2:8-13 NIV we are told not to believe the philosophy of human tradition, but to depend on the truth as it is in Christ. Sinful human tradition comes as a result of sinful nature. We are to die to our sinful nature and be raised with Christ into divine nature. "In Christ all the fullness of the Deity lives in bodily form, and you have been given fullness in Christ, who is the head over every power and authority. In him you were also circumcised, in the putting off of the sinful nature, not with a circumcision done by the hands of men but with the circumcision done by Christ, having been buried with him in baptism and raised with him through your faith in the power of God, who raised him from the dead."

And now let us look at Romans 1:1-4 NIV where Apostle Paul speaks further on the humanity and deity of Christ and what it means for us today. "Paul, a servant of Christ Jesus, called to be an apostle and set apart for the gospel of God – the gospel he promised beforehand through his prophets in the Holy Scriptures regarding his Son, who as to his human nature was a descendant of David, and who through the Spirit of holiness was declared with power to be the Son of God by his resurrection from the dead: Jesus Christ our Lord."

Concerning this passage of scripture, in his book, *Walking with Paul Through the Book of Romans*, Dr. Knight shows that Paul reminds us of the fact that Jesus is both human and divine. Jesus is the Son of David as well as Son of God. He is the son of Mary but not of Joseph. Therefore, Jesus is the son of Mary and the Holy Spirit. So now being both human and divine He positions Himself to save us from our sins, as "God with us." And as the "Son of David," He is the messianic promise spoken of in 2 Samuel 7:12, 13 to establish David's throne eternally.

The prophet Jeremiah later prophesied about this promise in Jeremiah 23:5, 6. Then in the New Testament, just before the birth of the Messiah, the prophecy is again given. In Luke 1:32 the angel of the Lord says to Mary, "He shall be great, and shall be called the Son of the Highest: and the Lord God shall give unto him the throne of his father David."

The prophet Isaiah in the Old Testament also prophesied concerning the promised Messiah. And in this prophetic word, he also reveals a very pertinent truth that needs to be disclosed here and now. This next text is an essential truth, the clincher. The truth found in this text will bring our study concerning the third Person of the Godhead together for us. Isaiah 53:1: "Who has believed our message, and to whom has the arm of the Lord been revealed?" This text has a twofold message. First, it speaks of the coming of the Messiah, whom God would send. Additionally it gives us the gender revelation of the "arm of Yahweh," the Holy Spirit. The word *message* comes from the Hebrew word *shemuwah*, meaning, something heard; news; tidings; report; or announcement. So the message includes both the revelation of Jesus Christ and also of the Holy Spirit. The original Hebrew text reads: "Who has believed the message of us, and the arm of Yahweh, whom *she* revealed?" And in this text the arm of Yahweh, the arm of God, the Holy Spirit is referred to as **SHE**.

John picked up on this Old Testament text and recorded it in the New Testament. He wrote, "This was to fulfill the word of Isaiah the prophet: 'Lord, who has believed our message and to whom has the arm of the Lord been revealed?' For this reason they could not believe. He has blinded their eyes and deadened their hearts, so they can neither see with their eyes, nor understand with their hearts, nor turn—and I would heal them.... Yet at the same time many even among the leaders believed in him.... But because of the Pharisees they would not confess their faith for fear they would be put out of the synagogue; for they loved praise from men more than praise from God" (John 12:37-42, NIV). Let me say that the "our message" found in John 12:38 and Isaiah 53:1 are the same words given to me as I completed the typing of the two dreams leading to this book. I had not yet seen this text when the words, "our message" were spoken to me.

We believe by faith that Jesus Christ is the Son of God, Son of the Father. In fact we believe that He is the "only begotten of the Father" (John 1:14). We also believe that the Son of God is not a created being, but rather, the Creator. So in the same way that we understand this truth, by faith, we should also understand that the Son of the Father is indeed the Son of Holy Spirit Mother as well. The Son of God, the second person in the holy Trinity, was not created but is Creator, just as the Holy Spirit and the Father are Creator. All three are Creator and none is the created; because each is God; and all are God. The "only begotten of the Father," is also "full of grace and truth" because the Holy Spirit is the Spirit of grace and the Spirit of truth (Hebrews 10:29 and John 16:13). Therefore we know that "In him dwelleth the fulness of the Godhead bodily" (Colossians 2:9).

Who is She?

In revealing the power of God, the work of the Holy Spirit, Jesus uses a particular phrase in John 11:43 that we will look at now. "He cried with a loud voice, 'Lazarus, come forth.'" During the time Jesus was on earth, in ancient Near Eastern culture, the role of midwifery was exclusively that of women. And during a difficult delivery of a child, the midwife would speak to the yet unborn child. She would call the child by name and command him to come forth. In similar fashion, Jesus, empowered by the Holy Spirit, calls dead Lazarus by name loudly and commands him to "come forth." And since John's theme focuses on the new birth as related to our spirituality, the story he records here emphasizes the work of the Holy Spirit as a womanly role. The spiritual leaders heard about this miracle method, and they then planned to kill Jesus (verse 53). Why?

Jesus visits the issue of who the Holy Spirit is with the Pharisees who were suggesting that His power to cast out demons came from Satan. Let us look at the texts: "And Jesus knew their thoughts, and said unto them, 'Every kingdom divided against itself is brought to desolation; and every city or house divided against itself shall not stand; and if Satan cast out Satan he is divided against himself; how shall then his kingdom stand? And if I by Beelzebub cast out devils, by whom do your children cast them out? Therefore they shall be your judges. But if I cast out devils by the Spirit of God [who is called the finger and hand of God in Luke 11:20], then the kingdom of God is come unto you. Or else how can one enter into a strong man's house, and spoil his goods, except he first bind the strong man? And then he will spoil his house. He that is not with me is against me; and he that gathereth not with me scattereth abroad. Wherefore I say unto you, all manner of sin and blasphemy shall be forgiven unto men: but the blasphemy against the Holy Ghost shall not be forgiven unto men. And whosoever speaketh a word against the Son of man, it shall be forgiven him: but whoever speaketh against the Holy Ghost, it shall not be forgiven him, neither in this world, neither in the world to come.... O generation of vipers, how can ye being evil, speak good things? For out of the abundance of the heart, the mouth speaketh.... But I say unto you, that every idle word that men shall speak, they shall give account thereof in the day of judgment. For by thy words thou shalt be justified, and by thy words thou shalt be condemned.... For whosoever shall do the will of my Father which is in heaven, the same is my brother, and sister, and mother" (Matthew 12: 25-37, 48-50).

If we look at the family throughout history, it is the wife—her safety and protection and then that of the children that any good husband is most concerned about. You can speak against him and even his children, but you'll be asking for even more trouble by speaking against or endangering his wife in any way. Father God and Holy Spirit Mother are also mutually protective. "Thy will be done on earth, as it in heaven." What you say against the Father's helper, help-meet and wife, Mother of God's only begotten Son, will either justify you or condemn you, according to verses 36 and 37 (also read John 10:36). They are the Holy Family. This entire chapter is loaded. Beginning with verse 25, Jesus is answering the Pharisees' question of His source of power. As we have already studied, His power came from His heavenly Mother, the Spirit of God. So Jesus answers them and uses an illustration of a family home situation in which robbers come in to steal from the home. To be successful, they must first bind up and incapacitate the husband, the strong man of the house. Then verses 31 and 32 follow with a warning against bothering the Holy Ghost. Why? It is because She is the Woman of the house, Holy Wife and Holy Spirit Mother. And if the spiritual thieves touch Her, or even speak against Her, they will never be forgiven. All manner of evil and blasphemy can be forgiven, but not blasphemy against the Holy Spirit.

Then looking at Matthew 12:40, we find Jesus responding to a request of his earthly mother, Mary, calling him to come out of the Temple so that she could silence his arguing with the people in there. It is interesting that Mary would come calling for her son at this particular time. Could it be that Mary, who was overshadowed, *hovered* and *moved upon* by the Holy Spirit to receive Jesus at incarnation, as surrogate mother, knew just what Jesus was trying to tell the people? Could it be that she thought the unveiling of and sharing with the people the fact that the Holy Spirit is Jesus' heavenly Mother, would cause tragic results for her son? Then add to that He was referring to Himself as the Son of God.

Jesus responded to such requests by His mother and siblings with: "Whosoever shall do the will of my Father which is in heaven, the same is my brother, and sister, and mother" (Matthew 12:50). Not only was He addressing and denying His earthly family's request while embracing the group of believers there, but on a higher level, a spiritual plain, He was holding to the fact that His heavenly Mother, the Holy Spirit, the Arm and Hand of God, carries out the will of His heavenly Father. And that She is the One who gives Him supernatural power to cast out the "works of darkness."

Acts 7:49-51. Now we could even more clearly see the connection, by comparing the previous dissertation of Jesus, with what God asks here: "Hath not my hand made all these things [Holy Spirit in creation from verse 49]? Ye stiff-necked and uncircumcised in heart and ears, ye do always resist the Holy Ghost; as your father did, so do ye. Which of the prophets have not your fathers persecuted? And they have slain them which showed before the coming of the Just One; of whom ye have been now the betrayers and murderers."

As we read earlier, the prophets of old, such as Isaiah and others, had foretold the coming of the Messiah. Prophet Isaiah in speaking of the One coming up as a "tender plant," meaning his growth and development as a human, also records the "arm of Yahweh" as "she" in the original Hebrew translation of the Bible. Isaiah predicts that the "arm of Yahweh", the Holy Spirit, would be revealed along with the Messiah. So the point here is that the New Testament refers back to the very verses of the Old Testament when referring to the Holy Spirit as female, and in connection to the Messiah. We see that John 12:37-42 refer back to the texts Isaiah 53:1-3. Also we see in John 10:25-38 where Jesus is referring to himself as the Son of God and speaks of the miracles he performs in the power of God, which we know as the power of the Holy Spirit.

Isaiah the prophet revealed the female identity of the Holy Spirit and prophesied of the coming Messiah. And he was murdered by evil Manasseh, a King of Israel in Old Testament times. It is said that Isaiah would not recant his statements of the Messiah, redemption of humankind and final judgment. I wonder whether the other statement, *arm of Yahweh* being *she,* have anything to do with his death too? Isaiah was willing to die for the sake of truth. What a courageous man.

Then, as we know, it was Manasseh's grandson, the tender eight-year old King Josiah, who was considered by God as a righteous king. Josiah ordered the man, Priest Hilkiah, to take the discovered book of the law to a woman, Prophetess Huldah, wife of Shallum, so that she could declare them authentic. God said that Josiah's heart was tender and that he was humble. He had no problem submitting to a woman of God, nor with obeying the Word of God. Therefore God allowed him to live and die in peace, before bringing judgment on Israel. We must become as little children, in humility and tenderness of spirit, if we are to see the kingdom of heaven. Please read this story in 2 Kings 22.

Finally, let us look in **John 16:12** at Jesus' interaction with His disciples before His crucifixion and ascension to heaven. We read that Jesus had some information and insight that He really wanted to share with them. Yet He perceived that His followers could not handle it at the time. Therefore we know that all revelation was not given to them. Some revelation knowledge has been held and is given as the Church matures spiritually. In His very next statement to the disciples He starts speaking of the Holy Spirit. In **verse 20** He says that they "shall weep and lament, but the world shall rejoice: and ye shall be sorrowful, but your sorrow shall be turned into joy." In **verse 21** He again picks up with a feminine activity of a woman "travailing in sorrow" which turns into joy after the birthing process is completed. I believe that one truth, among others, He really wanted to reveal to them, is that the Holy Spirit God is His heavenly Mother, but they weren't ready for it. Are we ready for it?

Scriptural facts concerning the Holy Spirit:

- The active life force at creation (Genesis 1:2).
- The active life force at Jesus' incarnation (Matthew 1:20).
- The active life force that led Jesus into the wilderness (Matthew 4:1).
- The source of Jesus' supernatural power (Luke 11:20).
- The active life force at Jesus' resurrection (Romans 8:11).
- The creative life force in our born again conversion experience (John 3:5-8).

- A mother who cares for and protects her babies (Numbers 11:2).

Shaddai is linked to the Hebrew word *shaddayim,* which means "breasts." In connection with the word *breast*, the term *Shaddai* (a feminine word) expresses the idea of the one who nourishes, sustains and satisfies. And connected with the word meaning God, *El*, El Shaddai then signifies the One who is mighty to pour forth nourishment, sustenance and blessing. Therefore, God is the God of abundance, according to the explanation set forth by Nathan Stone, in his book *Names of God.*

In *The IVP Women's Bible Commentary*, by Theologians Catherine Clark Kroeger and Mary J. Evans, we find that certain churches in ancient times used feminine terms in reference to the Holy Spirit until about 400 A.D.

In referring to the Holy Spirit, other clues to the feminine nature of God include:

- *Rehem* (Hebrew) means "womb of woman," and is linked with the concept of divine compassion.
- *Ru'ah,* "Holy Spirit," is a feminine word in original Hebrew.
- *Pneuma,* the Greek for "Holy Spirit", is a neuter word.
- The *Spirit of wisdom* is one of the titles of the Holy Spirit in the Bible. *Hokmah,* the Hebrew for *wisdom,* is a feminine word. S*ophia,* Greek for *wisdom* is a feminine word. The book of Proverbs refers to *wisdom* as *she.*
- A mother who gives birth to Israel. (Isaiah 46:3, 4).
- A mother who remembers her nursing child. (Isaiah 49:14,15).

- A mother who teaches, feeds, holds, and heals her children (Hosea 11:1-4).

Some additional Bible passages that reveal the femaleness of God as images and as in cultural activities include these:

- Job 38:8, 9
- Psalms 22:9,10; 71:6; 90:2; 123:2; 131:2.
- Proverbs 8:22-25
- Isaiah 31:5; 40:1-11; 45: 9-11; 66:7-14
- Nehemiah 9:20, 21
- Ruth 2:12
- Exodus 19:4
- Matthew 13:33
- Luke 13:20,21; 15:8-10
- Acts 17:28
- 1 Peter 2:2,3

Going back to the creation story again, we can even more clearly see the intended resemblance of God in the woman.

- *Eve* means, "mother of all living, life-giver." Therefore, a mother represents on earth what the Holy Spirit is in heaven. The words, "Thy will be done on earth as it is in heaven" came from the lips of God, the Son. This is that.
- The pronoun that God uses for "earth" is "she," according to the original Hebrew translation. The Spirit created the earth.
- The Bible calls the dust of the ground, from which Adam was scooped and formed by the hands of the Creator, "she." The original Hebrew translation reads: "Cursed is the ground because of you [Adam]. Through painful toil you will eat of *her* all the days of your life. *She* will produce thorns and thistles for

you, and you will eat the plants of the field. By the sweat of your brow you will eat your food until you return to the ground, since from *her* you were taken; for dust you are and to dust you will return" (Genesis 3: 17-19). The "he" man was taken from the "she" earth that was created by "She" Spirit.

Choose the Authentic or the Counterfeit

Let's review our discoveries:

- If you believe that the God family, the three-person triune Family created man and woman in Its image: "Let us make man in our image…male and female created he them";
- If you believe that God, the three of Them, made us with the intent that we look like and act like Them in image and likeness;
- If you believe that God created the institution of marriage and the family unit, and that the members in that marriage unit resemble and represent the members of the heavenly family of God;
- If you believe that Scriptures are the plan of God for individuals, for families, for churches, and establishments in the earth realm;
- If you believe that Jesus Christ gave us a model of hope and understanding in His prayer to His heavenly Father when He said, "Thy will be done on earth as it is in heaven";
- If you believe that God wants us to have the abundant life on earth for which Christ came and that our families should be as heaven on earth;

- If you believe that Jesus Christ is the Word made flesh, who by example, showed us the right attitude to have toward one another even though it may go against culture and tradition as shaped by sin and sinners;
- If you believe that the Holy Bible gives feminine attributes to the person and work of the Holy Spirit and refers to the Holy Spirit using feminine words in the original biblical manuscripts, and that modern translations have changed these to masculine words;
- If you can see that the ministry of the Holy Spirit in the spiritual realm perfectly parallels the work of a mother and woman in the earthly, human realm;
- If you believe that Jesus, the Son of God, who now sits on His heavenly throne, at the right hand of Father God, is coming back as King of kings and Lords of lords;
- If you believe that Jesus calls the church, His bride, a feminine image and does not call His church a warrior or a groom, masculine images, because He Himself is of the male gender;
- If you believe that a legal union between two persons of the same gender is not a legitimate marriage and cannot make up a legitimate family;
- If you believe that God ordained that it takes a man and a woman to make a marriage legitimate and authentic here on earth, because, "Thy will be done on earth as it is in heaven";

Then:

- You cannot and must not accept the insidious notion of two masculine counterparts in one heavenly Family.

- You cannot infer from the Bible that Father God, who is represented by the earthly father and husband, as well as Holy Spirit God, who is represented as the Help-meet of Father God, are both masculine.
- That would be two men and a son, an illegitimate family.
- That would not be right. And God would not have been just in torching Sodom and Gomorrah.
- So someone absolutely has to be the feminine God.

Why was God so displeased with Sodom and Gomorrah? Why such a stiff punishment for any righteous escapee just for looking back at the burning cities? Most theologians and teachers underscore the idea that looking back toward the cities represented being of the world or being worldly minded. Although this is a feasible explanation, it only scratches the surface.

I believe that here is the more in-depth and accurate explanation. Sodom and Gomorrah cities were controlled and populated by people who had a perverted view of family. They had adopted, propagated and celebrated a culture that made the natural role of the woman in companionship and authority, obsolete. They preferred families and systems that exalted man-man relationships above what the God family had created in Its own image and likeness.

We can read of the men refusing to accept the daughters that Lot offered them. These men had no use for women. It was the angels in male form that they longed to take to themselves. Lot's gesture of giving his daughters to the men, serves as a test case, a documentation of the wickedness and debasement of these men. God wanted to show the world what He thinks of this kind of culture and way of thinking. God ruled against these people who had embraced a counterfeit family system.

Therefore, when Lot, his wife and children, a legitimate family, were being guided to safety and his wife looked back, she was indicating her acceptance of the culture and customs of those cities. She could not bring herself to denounce what Sodom and Gomorrah stood for. Mrs. Lot had actually bought into the idea of a "men only" society, a male-dominated and male-preferred culture. She did not mind this anti-woman mindset as long as she was able to live comfortably with her own husband and family. As long as the ways of that culture did not directly affect her, she was willing to tolerate and even accept this system of sodomy. Therefore she was turned into a salt pole, a stationary, worthless, earth crystal incapable of moving forward. What she accepted and embraced, a misrepresentation of God and godliness immobilized her own progress and killed her.

And what about you and me? Have we thrown up our hands in acceptance of spiritual sodomy in order to continue to live comfortably in our own small existences? Have we joined or allowed organizations to flourish that promote gender preference and domination without pointing out the "thus saith the Lord"? Have we become useless salt poles unable to make progress?

Today do we embrace and long for what God is positioned to annihilate? Do you understand that gender preference in spiritual matters eventually leads to same-gender preference in social and physical matters? Is this why molestation of boys has been going on all these years in some churches and organizations? Is this why society today has so much trouble? Is this why we are now legalizing same-sex marriages?

The Bible speaks specifically to this issue. Let us look at the Holy Scriptures.

Romans 1:18-32. "For the wrath of God is revealed from heaven against all ungodliness and unrighteousness of men, who hold the truth in unrighteousness; because that which may be known of God is manifest in them; for God hath shewed it unto them. For the invisible things of him from the creation of the world are clearly seen, being understood by the things that are made, even his eternal power and Godhead; so that they are without excuse; because that, when they knew God, they glorified him not as God, neither were thankful; but became vain in their imaginations, and their foolish heart was darkened. Professing themselves to be wise, they became fools. And changed the glory of the incorruptible God into an image made like to corruptible man.... Wherefore God also gave them up to uncleanness through the lusts of their own hearts, to dishonor their own bodies between themselves; who changed the truth of God into a lie, and worshipped and served the creature more than the Creator, who is blessed forever. Amen. For this cause God gave them up into vile affections; for even their women did change the natural use into that which is against nature: And likewise also the men, leaving the natural use of the woman, burned in their lust one toward another; men with men working that which is unseemly, and receiving in themselves that recompense of their error which was meet. And even as they did not like to retain God in their knowledge, God gave them over to a reprobate mind, to do those things which are not convenient; being filled with all unrighteousness, fornication, wickedness, covetousness, maliciousness; full of envy, murder, debate, deceit, malignity; whisperers, backbiters, haters of God, despiteful, proud, boasters, inventors of evil things, disobedient to parents, without understanding, covenant-breakers, without natural affection, implacable, unmerciful: Who knowing the judgment of God, that they which commit such things are worthy of death, not only do the same, but have pleasure in them that do them."

Misinterpreting the Word of God and rejection of His Word will always lead to tradition that is not biblical. And tradition outside of truth will always lead to spiritual death and moral decay.

Since we agree that families comprised of two men and a child are not of God, and do not make up a legitimate family on earth, and that the earthly family was created to resemble and to reflect the God family, then who of the God family is the heavenly Mother? And if we believe that both male and female were created in God's image and likeness, what part of the Godhead, the Trinity, was the human female created to resemble and to pattern after?

What has been spelled out in the Holy Bible all of these thousands of years, even throughout female oppression eras and despite occasional limitations of culture-bound scriptural authors and despite gender word changes in modern translations of the Bible? It absolutely has to be the One with the feminine characteristics as laid out in the Word of God.

It is the One who is called the right hand of God, the arm of Yahweh, which represents God's Spirit. It is the One with the feminine roles. It is the One called "she" in Isaiah 53:1. It is God the Holy Spirit Mother.

God, the Father, is male.

God, the Son, is male.

God, the Holy Spirit, is female.

Hallelujah to the Living Word of God. Praise the Lord.

Come on brothers and sisters of salvation, men and women of the Word, friends of the gospel, children of Deity. Open your mind, and open your spirit. Think about it. Receive it. Believe it. Know it. Share it.

It does not matter what you have been told. It does not matter who told it to you. It does not matter what you thought. And it does not matter what you wish. The truth is that this truth has been here, all along. It has been screaming out in silence for millennia. Either we missed it, ignored it, or covered it up. But I praise Almighty God for the unveiling of it today!

This is revelation knowledge, recorded right here in the Bible, God's holy, accurate, applicable, and living Word.

This is God's revelation revolution.

Isaiah 48:16, NKJV: "Come near to Me, hear this: I have not spoken in secret from the beginning; from the time it was, I was there. And now the Lord God and His Spirit have sent me." This is the Old Testament prophet revealing the Trinity, and is referring to the pre-incarnate Christ and the *Ones ("the Lord God and His Spirit")* who sent Him here.

When you are able to understand that Holy Spirit God is a real being, just as you understand this concerning the Son of God, and Father God; when you understand that Holy Spirit God is a distinct personality in the God family rather than a mystical or abstract force, your paradigm, your existence, and your life will take a turn for the better in every way. Because then you can grasp the absolute truth that God created both male and female in His—Elohim (three Gods in one family), image and likeness, blessed them both, and gave both male and female dominion over the earth. We know that humankind did not receive blessing, dominion or the command for fruitfulness until the woman was made. After they were both created, then they were empowered to reach their full potential together, reflecting the image and likeness of God. God could not give the man dominion over the earth until the woman was made because the reflection of God was not complete in the man alone. God's reflection is complete in man and woman together. Not only did they resemble God in outward appearance but were made to resemble God in character as well. They were made to have lordship over the earth just as God, Elohim, rules the universe. Man and woman were given equal access to the earth as equal partners, representing heaven on earth. "Thy will be done on earth, as it is in heaven" (Matthew 6:10).

Learning the truth as recorded in God's Word and by comparing passage with passage in context and with an open spirit will change your life forever. It changed mine. It will change the way men and women interact. It will change the way women interact with other women. And it will change the way a woman "interacts" with herself. If you cannot grasp this concept, you may accept the false notion that only the male gender was created in God's image. Then you might also be inclined to conclude that dominion was given only to the male and that whatever the female obtains and how she exists on earth must come to her from a male counterpart. And if you believe that, then you would also be inclined to believe that the woman can only have the role of support and a sideline-cheering type of existence. And according to the Bible this idea is absolutely not true. This idea is not of God.

Let me just share a little piece of church history with you before we move on. Just as the deity of Christ has been debated, so has the deity of the Holy Spirit. Perhaps this is because the debaters had a hunch that God the Holy Spirit indeed is the feminine God.

It is believed that the bishop of Constantinople, Macedonius, during the time 341-360 A.D., submitted that the Holy Spirit was a servant of God similar to angels having a subordinate position to the Father and Son. This was a denial of the deity of the Holy Spirit. His teaching was condemned and rejected in 381 by the ecumenical Council of Constantinople. The Western churches have embraced the deity and person of the Holy Spirit as equal to that of the Father and the Son. There is more detail on this issue in the book, *Christianity Through the Centuries*, by Earl E. Cairns.

I believe that Father God and Holy Spirit Mother God, gave their only begotten Son to redeem our fallen human race. God sent forth His Word, just like in the beginning, at creation. Remember, "And God said (spoke His *Word*)"? "And the *Word* was made flesh, and dwelt among us" (John 10:10).

Chapter Five

Family Value

Divine DNA

How was the incarnation transformation accomplished? Who was the steward and the transporter of this divine DNA? It was the same "hovering One," and the One who overshadowed Mary, just like at Creation. Remember? The Spirit of the Lord overshadowed or hovered over Mary. "That which is conceived in her is of the Holy Ghost" (Matthew 1:20). Father God sent forth His Word, Jesus, which was carried by God's help-meet, the Holy Spirit. Let us look at the incarnation of Christ in a way that we can begin to understand this process within the confines of our human capacity. The Aramaic word for *overshadowed* as found in Luke 1:35 is *helek*. *Helek* means *a walk or journey*. It also means *a flowing* and *dropped*.

I believe that this is the way in which Christ's incarnation was accomplished. God the Father's holy Seed (Genesis 3:15), His Word (John 10:10), His Message and Report (Isaiah 53:1), was given to His helper, the Holy Spirit. And since this Son of God also had to become the Son of Man (a human being), the Holy Spirit had to find a "suitable helper" for Father God in the earth realm, just as Adam longed for a "suitable helper" in the beginning. A helper in the human race, a woman, was needed, through which Jesus could be born. So the Holy Spirit chose a handmaid that She could trust and use.

In ancient times it was customary for a wife who was barren to use her handmaid as surrogate mother. In this way a child could be born into the family as a legitimate heir. The woman's husband would plant his seed into the handmaid. During the birthing process, the wife would recline knee-to-knee with her handmaid. And at the time of delivery this wife and her husband would receive the child into the family as their very own.

This practice parallels, what happened with the Holy Spirit and Mary. The Holy Spirit, "unable" to bare a human son, chose Mary as surrogate mother. This was the way chosen for the Son of God to become the Son of Man. And this is why Mary said, "Behold the handmaid of the Lord; be it unto me according to thy word" (Luke 1:38). Mary understood her role. She understood her relationship with the Holy Spirit. It was a Woman to woman arrangement.

So the Holy Spirit overshadowed Mary to initiate creative change, to create order in place of disorder, this world of sin. This delicate procedure, on which the future of the world depended, was a great success. So the Holy Spirit took a *walk* to the dwelling place of Her handmaid, Mary. And there was *a flowing* into Mary—that which the Holy Spirit Mother brought from Father God. The Seed of God was *dropped* into the womb of Mary to combine with the seed of Mary, her genetic material.

In medical terms this was the first "artificial insemination" procedure, accomplished by God, the great Physician. Today this is a very common medical procedure used for overcoming certain infertility problems in families. Medical wisdom and all other wisdom come from our Creator. And therefore Immanuel, God with us, became reality. "For unto us a child is born, unto us a son is given… and his name shall be called Wonderful, Counselor, The mighty God, the everlasting Father, The Prince of Peace" (Isaiah 9:6). To understand the term "the everlasting Father" as it relates to Jesus, please review Hebrews 1. Jesus is the express image of His Father. Jesus told His disciple, Phillip, "He that hath seen me hath seen the Father" (John 14:9). Please read John 14:6-13 also. And now that the Son of God has been born into the human family, we also may become "heirs of God, and joint heirs with Christ." We are "heirs according to the promise." Please review Romans 8:17 and Galatians 3:29.

They Chose a Surrogate Mother

The Holy Spirit Mother deposited the Seed of God, into the womb of the surrogate mother, Mary. The God family used Mary and Mary's womb to connect with the human race. Joseph had nothing to do with that. That is why the Bible says in 1Timothy 2:15, that women are saved through childbearing. This simply means that through the female gender, the human race received salvation in Jesus Christ, who came to save His people from their sins.

Because of Adam's deliberate disobedience, as well as his refusal to take responsibility for his own choice of disobedience, his male seed was bypassed when the last Adam, Jesus, came to earth. God used the seed of the woman, as He promised in Genesis 3:15. He also said to the woman that here desire would be unto her husband

and that her husband would rule over her. Let's take a closer look at this.

He Became the Blamer

There are many different theories as to what Genesis 3:16b actually means. If you study the context of the conversation between God and the guilty couple after sin entered, I believe that you would understand and agree with this interpretation. Consider the following contextual interpretation. You see, since Adam blamed the woman for the sin problem, her "desire" was to take the blame and heat off of Adam, to bare it herself, since she had sinned first. The Father knew what she was feeling. And so He simply said that her desire would be to her husband (Genesis 3:16). In Strong's Exhaustive Concordance we see that the Hebrew word for desire is *tshuwqah*, which means a longing for, to stretch out after, to run after, to overflow. So this meaning is referring to the woman's emotional state concerning her relationship with her husband, as well as her overflowing with emotion. She longed for a growing and lasting relationship with her husband, and therefore would do or take anything for it—even the blame. We can see retrospectively that she exhibits a typical sign of abused wife syndrome in that she "went along to get along." The woman went along as blame bearer to get along with and to stay connected to her husband, the blamer.

But God also said that the man would rule over her. I believe the Father was saying: Woman, I know you want to take the blame since your husband is indeed blaming you, but if you let your emotions get the best of you, he is going to keep on blaming you forever.

God required the man to take the blame for his own bad choice and to suffer in providing for his family under the hardship of a cursed ground. And since he willfully sinned, he became the partner-provider, like a servant, who worked the fields under hardship to sustain himself and his family. As we know, biblical rulership also imposes the status and posture of a servant. Additionally, the "and he shall rule over thee" prophecy that God spoke to the woman was a warning that if she would allow her emotions to overflow, to get the best of her and influence her decisions, her husband would take that opportunity to rule over her in a sinful way—the opposite way of biblical rulership which is servanthood.

God did not say that the woman was not the man's equal anymore. You need to understand this fact. We have for so long been taught that the woman was "put under" the man because she sinned first. This is not biblical. The woman was doomed to pain in childbearing. That was the extent of her punishment, which she brought upon herself. But because her emotions were out of control, her "desire" got the best of her, she allowed the man to get away with making her bear the burden of the blame for sin, along with the implications of that. She was willing to go along with this emotional abuse, in order to maintain a close relationship with her husband. This is why, I believe, that motherhood and womanly roles are not celebrated, as God intended they should be in our world. Man has indeed placed himself above the woman in a sinful way; and the woman has allowed him to do this, being ruled by her emotions, her "desire."

As you well know, women with careers are viewed as being more successful and more significant than women who carry out child rearing and in-home responsibilities. Because the man was given the responsibility of provider-servant-partner, and because of the attitude of men concerning the woman having caused the sin problem, then any womanly role would become the lesser significant role in the eyes of those men and women who buy into this belief system. This is the male's coping device for his provider and servant position imposed by God after sin. He has changed the intent of God's punishment on his manly position as provider-servant-partner to that of superior partner and ruler over the woman. And also attached to this kind of thought process, is that when a woman decides to get an education and pursues a career, as she well should, she is often discounted and devalued by competing male colleagues simply because she is a woman. Additionally she endures many struggles and challenges in order to arrive at a place of achievement and dominion. The well known phrase, "It's a man's world," describes this kind of traditional attitude toward the woman.

Sinful tradition has taken differences between gender characteristics and has then used these differences against women. But as women have begun taking on additional roles, we find that they have been and continue to be significant contributors in society. God planned that both the man and the woman equally live up to their full potential as contributors and leaders in the world. And according to the Word of God, this planet was created for both "male and female" alike. A best-selling author, Dr. Miles Monroe discusses this in his book, *Understanding the Purpose and Power of Woman.*

Now let us look at the name "Eve." So far in this chapter I have referred to the first created female as "the woman." And here is why. At creation God gave the name "Adam" and "man" to both the male and the female. According to Genesis 5:2 KJV, God "called their name Adam, in the day when they were created." God's name for the male and the female was "Adam." There was Adam-man and Adam-woman, or Adam-male and Adam-female. The root meaning of the word *adam* means *human beings of the earth.* They were both made from the dust of the earth and were both given dominion over the earth from which they were made.

The first mention of the word "Eve" comes after sin entered the family unit and after the pronouncing of the curses. In Genesis 3: 20, we find that "Adam called his wife's name Eve; because she was the mother of all living." Here is the second critical turning point of gender relations after sin. The first point was Adam-man's finger pointing at the woman. The name that the God family gave to both man and woman, *Adam,* was the name they were supposed to have. This name, Adam, meaning *of the earth*, was tied into the blessing, the command for fruitfulness, multiplication and dominion of the earth.

After sin, the man retained the name Adam. But he renamed the woman, giving her the name, Eve. In doing so, he fulfilled God's prophetic word to the woman that her husband would rule over her. The man, by retaining his God-given name continued in the mindset of blessing, fruitfulness, multiplication *and* having dominion over the earth. By renaming the woman, he limited her to the role of multiplying only. Eve means, *mother of all living.* So multiplying and mothering became her only value, the man's definition of womanhood. When Adam-woman accepted this renaming, she accepted Adam-man's reassignment for her life, her value and essence.

Why didn't Adam-man name Adam-woman "Eve" when she was presented to him? In their perfect state of sinlessness, why didn't the name "Eve" come to his mind as the appropriate name for his wife? When Adam-man renamed Adam-woman after sin, he did so in the context of revaluing her. He re-evaluated her significance, essence and position in the family unit and in the society they would create together. He rearranged the order that God had ordained at creation. He repositioned her status to a place beneath his. This was all based on his attitude that the woman was the problem, the blame and reason for his sinful situation. This rearrangement and reassignment of the woman's God-given position on earth has been passed on throughout every generation since then. It is a result of sin and of fear resulting from sin. It has been man's answer to God's question of his sinfulness—"The woman whom thou gavest to be with me, she gave me of the tree, and I did eat." Strained gender relations is a spiritual matter. Male-superiority ideation is man's answer to God's question concerning his spiritual deficiency.

Jesus Christ is called the "last Adam." He came to give the woman a rebirth to renew her rightful status, value, arrangement and position here on earth. That is why He said, "Ye must be born again." When you receive rebirth in Christ, the old traditional issues are passed away. All become new. And in this state of spiritual innocence, the woman will remember her original God-given identity, and pattern her life after the heavenly Model. This is the only way one can see and enter the kingdom of God. The kingdom is among us. And for those reborn, the kingdom of God is within us. Only then can we see life the way God sees it. Only then can we live the way God intended from the beginning. Please review John 3:1-21.

Cyclical Reminder Established

Since Adam-man blamed God and Adam-woman for his own disobedience, God told the woman that through *her seed*, not through the man's seed, the Redeemer would come to bruise the head of the serpent— defeat Satan. This was a covenant promise God made with the woman, a blood covenant. Through the Seed of the woman, sin would be conquered.

"And without shedding of blood" there is no remission of sin (Hebrews 9:22). The blood of God's Son, the Lamb of God, would have to be shed for the redemption of humankind, in order to bring us back into right relationship with the God family. Just as the rainbow speaks of God's post-flood promise, I believe that the menstrual cycle of the woman speaks of God's post-sin promise concerning the coming Messiah, the woman's Seed. The "shedding of blood" certainly foremost refers to the blood of the spotless "Lamb of God, which taketh away the sin of the world" (John 1:29). But because of the chosen process through which He would come into our human race, it also refers to the monthly "shedding of blood" cycle. There is no childbirth without the female's reproductive cyclical activity. And there is no childbirth without blood at delivery. Through the woman's reproductive system, the Christ-child would enter the human family. Therefore in the book of Leviticus we read about ceremonial laws having to do

Just as the rainbow speaks of God's post-flood promise, I believe that the menstrual cycle of the woman speaks of God's post-sin promise concerning the coming Messiah, the woman's Seed.

with the woman's monthly shedding of blood from the womb, the menstrual cycle. In the Levitical system the woman was considered ceremonially unclean, in that the husband could not have sexual relations with her during this time. And in like manner, Joseph could not have sexual relations with his wife, Mary, until after the birth of the Messiah. Aside from the hygienic, health, and fertility reasons that are beyond the scope of this book, I believe that there were psychological and spiritual implications for which the husband had to keep his distance during his wife's monthly shedding of blood, menstrual activity.

Being ceremonially unclean directs one "to be careful" and "to give special attention." God wanted to reintroduce and to ever remind human beings of the covenant He had made with the woman; and that the man was not to interfere or have an intimate part with His arrangement. It is a sacred time, a prophetic event, a God-to-woman memorial. And I believe that for this reason women were not required to physically offer animal sacrifices to God in the Tabernacle service system. The sacrificing of the lamb, as we know, pointed to the spotless Lamb of God, the coming Messiah who would pay the penalty once for all. Since a role of woman is life-giver, and Redeemer conduit, it would be inappropriate for the life-giver to serve as life-taker.

Requiring the male person to do this act of killing the lamb served to remind the man of his participation in the sin problem and of his responsibility. Women served in other offices of the worship services just as men did. But they were spared the duty of killing the sacrificial lamb. And since the Lamb of God has been sacrificed, He alone is our High Priest "who also maketh intercession for us" (Romans 8:4). We do not need an earthly high priest to get to God's throne room anymore. In fact, we as believers are seated with Christ in heavenly places (Ephesians 2:6). Hallelujah. And all believers, both male and female are God's chosen people who serve as priests unto the Lord, interceding for those living in darkness of sin. The Apostle Peter puts it this way, "But ye are a chosen generation, a royal priesthood, an holy nation, a peculiar people; that ye should shew forth the praises of him who hath called you out of darkness into his marvelous light" (1 Peter 2:9). So there is no such position as "priest of the home" often used to refer to husbands. As believers in Christ, we are all priests unto the Lord.

Understand the Spiritual Accountability

God certainly could have used man's seed. The angel certainly could have appeared to Joseph and said that God would overshadow him and implant a special seed into him which he would then implant into his wife, Mary, to bring forth the Son of God. But God did not do this. Jesus Christ, the "last Adam", came through Mary's seed. The man, the male gender, represented by Joseph, was excluded. He was included later as a vessel of provision and protection of the woman, Mary and of the Christ child.

In the New Testament we see that the husband is the head of the wife the way Jesus is the head of His wife, the bride-church. In Mark 9:35 God explains this rulership role by saying, "If any man desires to be first (head, ruler, lord) the same shall be last of all, and servant of all." Here the Father defines *rulership*. And that is exactly what Jesus modeled while establishing the Church, His bride, on earth. He showed exactly what rulership is all about. "He humbled Himself unto death, even the death of the cross." Jesus, as Head of the church, willingly became sin for her. He took the blame of which He had no part; and He did not condemn her even though she was guilty of sin.

We have established from the Genesis record that Adam-man willfully sinned but made Adam-woman take the blame for them both. Jesus came to earth and did exactly the opposite of what Adam did. So now, read Genesis 3:16 in the light of Jesus' actions toward His bride. Once we understand what happened in the Garden of Eden the way God saw it, we will begin to understand the spiritual accountability of the man, as well as his provider-servant position. Satan has completely misled the human race into perverting what God intended for the family. Thus, most families on earth are dysfunctional. Sin has poisoned the root. Until we accept the truth as it is in the Word, the prevailing misinterpretation of the problem, punishment, promise, process, and prophecy concerning the man and the woman will hold us in the grip of falsehood.

God certainly could have used man's seed. The angel certainly could have appeared to Joseph and said that God would overshadow him and implant a special seed into him which he would then implant into his wife, Mary, to bring forth the Son of God. But God did not do this. Jesus Christ, the "last Adam", came through Mary's seed. The man, the male gender, represented by Joseph, was excluded.

Because of sin, the family unit has not rightfully recognized nor reflected God's image and likeness. It takes both male and female together, unified, to complete that reflection. Sinful tradition says that the female has no such identity with God and is not represented in the Godhead. It says that there are only masculine figures in the God family. Therefore, the family structure has no stable foundation. It is uneven and lopsided. This is why the very core of the family unit is faulty at best. The family can only be restored, when the image of God is restored within the family. "Thy will be done on earth as it is in heaven." After sin entered the family unit in Eden, the shining glory surrounding the beautiful body of Adam-man and Adam-woman disappeared. Then they became ashamed of their nakedness. Which parts of their body were they ashamed? Were they ashamed of their faces, hands, toes, ankles or what? They felt the shame of their reproductive organs being exposed—just like today. Why? Because these body parts reflected their difference as male and female and also represented each one's identity with a member of the Godhead. These parts of the human body represent the masculinity and femininity of God. And it is here that Satan has been most successful in his attack against the family unit.

In their spiritual innocence Adam-man and Adam-woman, wrapped in shekinah glory, felt no sense of shame. *Shekinah* is a feminine Hebrew word for the presence or heavy presence of God. Glory means splendor, and manifestation of God's presence. The Holy Spirit is called the glory of God (1Peter 4:14). The woman is called the glory of her husband (1Corinthians 11:7). And as we have seen, Holy Spirit is the feminine God. Holy Spirit Mother, Creator of Adam-man and Adam-woman, was present with them in their spiritual innocence.

And as Mother, the son and daughter felt no shame in their nakedness. Just as any child who is naked before his/her mother, there is absolutely no shame. The mother is familiar with the child's nakedness. The mother embraces the child's nakedness. The mother has godly love for the child's nakedness. The mother knows the child's nakedness. She bore her child in its nakedness. The child does not think about fig leaves for covering; there is no shame. The child does not think about running to hide from Mother's presence; there is no shame. Only after sin wedged itself between Mother and children, Adam-man and Adam-woman saw themselves as naked, and became fearful and ashamed.

The First Wife Abuser

As I said near the beginning of this book, the awful results of sin have been all pervasive and all inclusive. Adam-woman was not the only person deceived. Adam-man was also deceived in that he believed what Satan told him. He believed that the woman was at fault for his own choice to sin. He actually bought into such a bold lie and became the first wife abuser. He emotionally and verbally violated the wife that he had just recently congratulated himself for her having been made of his own flesh and bone.

After the couple sinned, God called out to Adam-man and Adam-woman. He asked where they were. God asked them to give an account of their shamefulness, deficiency and guilt. Unlike the silence he exhibited at the forbidden tree just moments earlier, Adam-man spoke up quickly. And even at that, he did not speak up in order protect his wife. He verbally blamed her for his sin. And he blamed God for giving him the woman who "caused" him to sin.

There is no wonder why the God family then chose to connect with Adam-woman, instead of with Adam-man, in bringing the Son of God, the "last Adam" into the world. God deliberately left the male out of the process of providing this level of redemptive provision required by His plan. The decision was specifically in response to the wrong attitude and abuse the man had exhibited toward his wife as well as to his own willful disobedience. This is why the bible also says that a husband who mistreats and disrespects his wife hinders his own prayers to God (1 Peter 3:7). God does not want husbands to mistreat wives, nor wives husbands.

The same kind of sinful attitude that Adam-man harbored against Adam-woman has been perpetuated through his male bloodline against the female, even to the present time. So the woman became devalued, discounted and generally disenfranchised. This is exactly why we find in Genesis 4:19 and 23 that Lamech, Adam's sixth generation grandson, took two wives instead of one. He felt that one woman was not sufficient because of the reassigned value placed on her by the male gender. Lamech later became a murderer. Devaluation of human life followed devaluation of the human female.

We can see that these attitudes still prevail today in many ways. Unfortunately, some men still find masculinity in blaming women for their own problems, deficiencies and guilt. This is why female gender discrimination, as well as all other forms of abuse against women, still run rampant today. In cases of abuse, the wife, girl-friend, daughter, female worker, female student, female church member, etc. are targets of the sin-sick soul of some men in their life. And many of these emotionally, physically, or sexually abused women have a "desire" to bear the blame and burden of the abuse, in order to preserve the relationship or membership. The statistics of domestic violence, where women are abused, are staggering. Please take time to look into this issue for yourself—the vast lists and details cannot fit into this book.

Another abomination I should mention here is that of clitoral mutilation practiced in some cultures. In order for a female, coming into her womanhood, to be accepted and considered a worthy citizen and a person worth marrying, there is a religious ritual that requires the young woman to have her clitoris excised, with or without her freely given consent. After this painful, humiliating and horrible procedure is done to her, she is now ready to be a "fit" wife and an acceptable citizen. What God has created for her good, and for the good of the family unit, the tradition of man has rejected and decided to cut out, so that the woman, now "recreated" by the man, is fit to partner with him both maritally and socially. Can you see the underlying deception here? This thought process and violent tradition is an affront to the creative genius of the Creator. God already made the woman "fit" for the man and for this earth. Man is stepping way out of line by mutilating and rejecting what God has set in place. This belief system is a perpetuation of traditional ideation handed down Adam's bloodline. It all starts with an attitude and eventually manifests as physical and social violations.

And in many of the domestic violence cases occurring today, the woman's emotions lead to bad decisions. Her "desire," her emotional disposition, leads her to rationalize reasons for her abuse. Her desire to continue in relationship with her abuser outweighs the common sense decision to report or to end the abusive relationship. In many cases she actually believes that such abuse was caused by something she did, said, or wore. She allows the abuser to get away with this aggression while she bears the blame, the pain and the shame.

But as you know, God did not create the woman for such purpose. And this is completely against the will of God. Sin is a state of mind that is followed by ungodly actions.

When God asked Adam, "Where art thou?" He was simply reaching out to the fallen family. He, of course, already knew where Adam was and what had been done. Adam-man read God's intent of inquiry as a call of condemnation. And his reply was a projection onto God and onto his wife what sin had created within his own heart. And it was out of this fear, this embarrassment and shame that he accused God and the woman for his condition. Fear is from Satan. Fear is a product of sinfulness. Love is from God, because "God is Love" (1 John 4:16).

God's love-search for Adam was simply a prophecy that the Son of God would one day come to earth to "seek and save that which was lost" (Luke 19:10). Adam-man replied to God's call in an attitude of blaming and renaming.

Adam-man sinned willfully. Adam-woman fell to the trickery of Satan while Adam-man stood by. The woman did not blame God for her actions, nor Adam's silence; she did blame the snake for tricking her (Genesis 3: 12, 13). Because Adam-man blamed God and the woman, God chose to partner with the woman and to use the seed of the woman in bringing redemption to mankind. Galatians 4: 4-6 says it this way, "But when the fullness of time was come, God sent forth His Son, *made of a woman*, made under the law, to redeem them that were under the law, that we might receive the adoption of sons. And because ye are sons, God hath sent forth the Spirit of His Son into your hearts, crying 'Abba, Father.'" This word "sons" means children, both male and female in the original Greek. It is an all inclusive word.

In verses 24-31 God contrasts the children of the world, symbolized as those born of Hagar, to the children of the promise, born of Sarah. Here the children of the promise are paralleled with the children of God, born of the Holy Spirit, the Divine Mother.

So Jesus' earthly existence began in Mary's womb in the form of human fetal life. With His divinity set aside, she bore him into the human family and raised him as a member of the human race. As the Holy Spirit guided Mary, she guided her child, Christ. "And Jesus increased in wisdom and stature, and in favor with God and man" (Luke 2:52).

The holy family of God became part of the sinful human family through the birth and life of Jesus. Then the human family became part of the holy family of God through the death and resurrection of Jesus. He is our triune connection!

The holy family of God became part of the sinful human family through the birth and life of Jesus. Then the human family became part of the holy family of God through the death and resurrection of Jesus. He is our triune connection! Praise God Almighty.

Does it Matter?

Now that we have biblically proven that the Holy Spirit is female. Let me say a few things about this. A male friend asked me some interesting questions about this subject. He asked, "Why is it important that the Holy Spirit is female? I mean, so what? What does it matter?" These are the questions that I have been asked by men who cannot dispute the Scriptures presented to them concerning the feminine God. I respond to all such questions, with the following questions:

- Is it important to you that the Holy Spirit *not* be female? If so, why?
- If it doesn't at all matter to you one way or another, why ask those first questions anyway?
- Perhaps somewhere in these following questions, is the answer to your question:
- Why is it important to you that your children look like you?
- Why do we have and use paternity testing?
- Why is it important to you that you, in some way, resemble members of your family?
- Why do we have, need, and make families.
- Why is it important to have role models?
- Why do the works of artists relate and reflect the time, place, people, and culture in which they live?
- Why do educational books, television shows, publications, media, music, and all forms of communication, documentation, and historical records create images specifically designed to represent and to meet the identity needs of its audience?
- Why are toys, such as dolls and action figures, made to represent different ethnicities and genders for children to play with?
- Why was it important to Adam and to God that Adam find a suitable helper, completer of the whole and not just any helper, like a zebra or a bird? With God all things are possible.

- Is it a God-given quality to desire and appreciate identity? Is it a God-given quality to have meaningful connection, to be a part of the whole, to fit into and to be a contributor of purpose, activity, and existence?
- Is it true that where there is no identity and no connection, there is no real interest and no celebrated value? Is that why Father God and Holy Spirit Mother, send Their only Son, Jesus, to restore us to our rightful place in the heavenly family?
- Why is God a family?
- And if your search for answers has not produced an answer for the "why female" question, do you persist in believing that the Godhead family is a three male family unit? If so, why?
- Why did God beget a son? And why did God make male and female in the image and likeness of the God family?

"If there be any virtue, and if there be any praise, think on these things" (Philippians 4:8).

God is male and female, father and mother; because God is Trinity, three personalities in one family. Celebrating God as masculine only, while assigning the feminine to the flesh and sinfulness, is idolatry because it translates into man worshipping his maleness, instead of his Creator, God.

When the woman understands who she is, how and why she was created, who her model is, and whom she is to represent, she will also understand how to live her life here on earth within the family and in society.

During my research I learned that throughout the first five books of the Bible, feminine nouns and verbs referring to God have been changed to masculine forms or have been deleted or otherwise concealed from its reader. These were deliberate efforts on the part of those wanting to devalue the female image and conceal the truth of the female God. As one such example, let us look at Deuteronomy 32:18: "Of the Rock that begat (fathered) thee thou art unmindful, and hast forgotten God that formed thee." Here the word *begat*, means *fathered*, a masculine role. And the word *formed* does not reflect a gender term. Yet the original Hebrew translation reads like this: "You deserted and forgot God… the One bearing you," reflecting feminine activity. The NIV reads like this: "You deserted the Rock, who fathered you; you forgot the God who gave you birth." The NIV is an accurate translation from the Hebrew in this case, and includes both Father God and Mother God. But the KJV totally conceals the feminine noun and verb referring to God. This deeply set tradition has been perpetuated in religion globally. God knew this would happen and warned against it in Revelation 22:18 and 19. Please read it now.

When the woman understands who she is, how and why she was created, who her model is, and whom she is to represent, she will also understand how to live her life here on earth within the family and in society.

This generation needs to make deliberate efforts in bringing the system of inequitable tradition to an end. It is a spiritual stronghold that must be pulled down. We have already read what the Word of God says about those who suppress the truth. Please review Romans 1:18-32.

Press to the Front

I take our three little children to the toy store about twice a month for a "well done" celebration. On one recent trip, Walesia II was set on choosing her first Barbie doll. She found the Barbie section and shelf, but I noticed her pushing the dolls aside and looking deeper through the line-up near the back of the shelf. As I approached she said, "Mother, I'm looking for a Barbie doll that looks like me. Can you help me find one?" Then she saw a few on the back row. "Why are my kind on the back row?" She asked. Then she added, "If they were alive, they could press their way to the front where they belong, where I could see them like the others. I'm not going to get this doll until the people who stacked them put them on the front row where they belong."

If we would just translate this concept to the issue concerning the woman. There are those who have placed women in the back row of society, especially in the religious setting. The woman has been placed—shoved—into the lonely corner, behind the scene, fixed and forgotten, into a place of silence and obscurity, at the bottom of the significance barrel.

I appeal to the inner strength of every woman in such a predicament and to every man who values her. Come alive. Wake up. Shake off this paralyzing slumber. Press, press, press your way to the forefront of life, where the action is and where the light shines, where you can be seen and heard, counted, and chosen. Do not stay hidden. Do not permit your life to be tucked away in darkness and silence like lifeless dolls. Awake, arise, shine and move forward in the name of Jesus. In John 11:25, Jesus says, "I am the resurrection and the life." And "I am come that they might have life, and that they might have it more abundantly" (John 10:10). You have been called by God to be a living "epistle, known and read by all men" because in Christ, you and I are "more than conquerors" (2 Corinthians 3:2 and Romans 8:37).

Move out of the shadows and into God's marvelous light. The only shadow women need to be under is "the shadow of the Almighty" (Psalms 91:1). Any other shadow ensures their obscurity and not their safety.

Move out of the shadows and into God's marvelous light. The only shadow women need to be under is "the shadow of the Almighty" (Psalms 91:1). Any other shadow ensures their obscurity and not their safety.

Chapter Six

Family Education

Jesus' water baptism and 40-day wilderness experience of temptation, fasting, and prayer marked the transition from His human work as a carpenter to His spiritual work as Savior of the world. He left his carpenter father's workshop to go into His heavenly Father's world shop. He went from repairing furniture to repairing lives. He went from building cabinets for Father Joseph to building the Spiritual Kingdom for Father God.

Jesus left Mother Mary's care to live in His Holy Spirit Mother's care. So He went from one mission to the other mission, from Mother Mary's guidance to Holy Spirit Mother's guidance. When Jesus was baptized in the Jordan River, the Bible says that the Holy Spirit descended upon him in the form of a peaceful dove. So at His baptism two members of the Triune Family were present, Mother and Son.

He Turned His Plate Down

Then Father God's voice pierced the sky, saying, "This is my beloved Son, in whom I am well pleased." And that makes three.

After baptism and affirmation by His heavenly Father, the Holy Spirit led Jesus into the wilderness where He fasted and prayed. And there Satan tempted Him.

There are times in our lives that victory is gained and power is received only through prayer and fasting. Present your body a living sacrifice from time to time. Show God that you want Him more than you want food. Food is good, and I love good food. But I have learned to turn my plate down sometimes. I want God more than food. I want revelation knowledge more than food. I want supernatural power more than food. I want heavenly blessings more than food. I want divine guidance more than food. I want to eat the Bread of Life and drink Living Water more than I want a home cooked meal. I want to eat from the hand of the Master Chef. Oh how delicious. Glory hallelujah.

There are times in our lives that victory is gained and power is received only through prayer and fasting.

A mother teaches her children in the home and home school system. She equips the children with what they need to interact properly with the world around them. She tells them, shows them, and teaches them just who they are. The home had been Mother Mary's classroom; the wilderness became Holy Spirit Mother's classroom. So, Jesus was led into the wilderness by the Holy Spirit to teach, equip, and empower Him for His interaction with the world of darkness.

In much the same way, the Spirit of God teaches us the Word of God. She teaches us how to interact with the world around us. She teaches us how to handle bullies, too. The Word says, "Resist the devil, and he will flee from you" (James 4:7). In the wilderness Jesus encountered the biggest bully, Satan. He stood on the Word of God to defeat the enemy. He resisted temptation with "It is written." We too can be overcomers of evil by the power of the Holy Spirit within us and by the Word of the Lord, called the "sword of the Spirit" (Ephesians 6:17). "Not by might, nor by power, but by my spirit, saith the Lord of hosts" (Zechariah 4:6).

Luke 2:40 NIV says, "And the child grew and became strong; he was filled with wisdom, and the grace of God was upon him." Jesus was under Mary's care initially.

Then Luke 4:1 says, "And Jesus being full of the Holy Ghost returned from Jordan, and was led by the Spirit into the wilderness." Then at the end of his 40 days in the wilderness, we read that, "Jesus returned to Galilee in the power of the Spirit" (Luke 4:14). His ministry began, and the rest is history and herstory.

I would like to share a speech with you that came to me one afternoon as I went about my weekend chores. My daughter learned the speech and has had the opportunity to share with multitudes of people from different parts of the world. It is entitled, "Mother."

Mother

I would say that a mother is a woman who has had a baby. I think we all can agree that this is true. However, it is only a part of the meaning of *mother*. Using an acronym, let us explore the more complex concept of mother.

M is for the mother's maternal instinct. Through physical and spiritual bonds to her children, she is well able to take good care of them.

O is for offering herself as a living sacrifice and for the opportunity she takes to raise her children in the fear of the Lord.

T is for the tenderness with which she loves and cares for her family and for all others whom God sends her way.

H is for the Holy Spirit's anointing. Mother wakes up early in the morning to meet with Her. The power she receives nicely takes her through the entire day.

E is for energy and enthusiasm to educate her young in lessons of life and of eternity.

R is for reverence, the deep respect she has for God. R is for readiness to always do her best. And R is for the reward that awaits her on that Great Day.

We are thankful for and give tribute to mother.
If I were a Hispanic child, I would say, *"Muchas gracias."*
If I were Italian, I would say, *"Miaria grazie."*
If I were French, I would say, *"Merci beaucoup."*
If I were a Nigerian, child I would say, *"Oshe."*
If I were Chinese, I would say, *"M goi."*
If I were Vietnamese, I would say, *"Cam ong."*
If I were German, I would say, *"Danke schon."*
And if I were a deaf/mute child, I would say, (*She uses sign language here.*).
But being an all-American child, born in Washington, D.C., and also born of the Holy Spirit, I say today:
Hallelujah! Thank You, Almighty God, *Adonai.*
Thank You, Eternal One, Ebenezer, Emmanuel, *Elohim*, *El Shadai.*
Thank You, *Yahweh, Jehovah Jirah.*
Thank you, my Living Water, my Storm Calmer, my Ailment Healer, my Mind Fixer, my Prayer Answerer. Savior of my soul!
For You, oh Lord, are the great Mother of the universe!
And all of Her children shall say: "Amen and amen again. Praise the Lord!"

Do Something With This Woman, Lord!

Jesus' life was a testimony to His home training. As much as He saw compliance with cultural negativity on the city streets, none of the customs influenced Him. As bad as it was back in those days for women and children, Jesus was never indifferent, condemning, or intolerant of them—not ever. There were times when even His disciples tried to keep women and children from "bothering" Jesus. But Jesus didn't allow it. Instead, He interacted with these people in a tender way and showed everyone that He valued them. In Mark 10:14 NIV Jesus said to those who were blocking others from Him: "Let the little children come to me; and do not hinder them, for the kingdom of God belongs to such as these."

I have been told through the years that there are places where a woman is considered to be a bad person after being raped by a man. She may be beaten, burned, or even killed, by her kinsman or a hired person, for bringing shame to the family. She is victimized for being a victim.

There are places on earth today, I am told, where men are legally allowed to beat women with sticks or other blunt objects. There are many, many statistics one can find about legal domestic violence, both in books and on the Internet.

There are places on this earth today where people believe a raped woman had worn her dress too short or had been where she should not have been. So it is her fault according to their thinking. They want to think that a woman should be blamed for violent aggression against her.

A favorite story of mine is recorded in John 8:1-11. Let's turn there. A woman was caught in the very act of adultery. It is probable that she was a married woman, because of the type of death sentence chosen. If she were a single woman, death by strangulation would have been the order of the day. It is said that the men had set her up for a fall in order to trap Jesus into saying something for which they could condemn Him. This kind of action exhibits displaced aggression. These men really had a problem with Jesus, the

Son of God. But in order to get at him they were willing and ready to trap, hurt and even kill a woman. Being angry with Jesus of whom they were fearful, they took out this anger on a little lady. Sounds familiar? This is what sinful tradition against women is all about. Adam-man, out of fear and shamefulness, especially after the favor shown to his wife by God concerning her seed of redemption, exhibited displaced aggression by devaluing her and placing himself "above" her in a sinful way. Adam-man was really angry with God. Jesus Christ came to this earth to undo what Adam and his descendants have done to women. And that is exactly what Jesus did, even in this particular situation. This mob dragged this woman out of her room, through the streets, and into the Temple court, bringing her to Jesus. Public humiliation followed by a sporty execution with rocks and a target (her body) was the plan for this lady.

Jesus was there in the Temple, teaching a group of people, on the eighth day of the Feast of Tabernacles. But of course He didn't just so happen to be there. His presence there was ordained by Holy Spirit Mother, so that He could stand for the right, which was a stand against the wrong. His stand for the right was recorded for present and future generations. The Spirit of God knew that we would need a "today Word" to understand the mind of the triune God family concerning women. Not by what we have been told, not by what we wish, not by what we just thought and not by what sinful tradition demands, but by the holy Word of Almighty God.

What would Jesus say? Well, let's see. Here was a woman caught in more or less voluntary, illicit sexual behavior, and with a man, I might add. Yet Jesus did not condemn her to violence, humiliation, or death. What a difference Jesus makes in our lives!

Here Jesus is on the scene, teaching in the Temple court. The men brought the woman to Him and set her in the midst of the crowd. Perhaps someone also brought a sack of rocks for the execution.

What did the mob do with the woman's sexual partner? Where was he? Had he been instructed to go home and shower, then return quickly for the sporty execution of this woman? Based on what they had seen, or had not seen, the mob had already judged and convicted this woman, while pardoning the adulterous man. I am so glad that although man looks on the outward appearance, God looks on the heart (1 Samuel 16:7). Jesus saw passed this woman's sin and saw her need of forgiveness, protection and direction.

This course of action without investigation was not new to these people. Remember the story found in the Old Testament about Hannah in the Temple? I find it interesting that the prophet Samuel is the person to whom God told this story for documentation in His book. Eli, the priest, accused Samuel's mother of being drunk when she was simply begging the Lord to give her a child. This woman was already in despair about her barrenness. Then added to that, she was falsely accused by a man of God. The good thing about Priest Eli was that after he had been corrected by Hannah and saw his fleshly error, he apologized and blessed her. You can read this story in 1 Samuel 1.

Beware of Modern Mob Mongers

What reaction to correction would a modern man or church leader have today in the same kind of situation? There are women today who are hurting and are in despair. They do what they know to do in order to cope and to gain victory over their situation. They are at times mistaken as being "misled" and labeled "trouble makers." But God is listening to such women, and He will answer. Remember, Priest Eli was later judged, by God, for not correcting his own sons for their very obvious evil activities. Why did Eli not correct his own sons for the horrible abominations they continuously committed, but very quickly accused this woman for something that proved to be untrue? When God gets fed up with inequities and inconsistencies, He steps in and judges the offenders. Think on this for a minute. Read about what happened to Eli's sons and then to Eli. Read about the reason and the ways he and his sons met with death. And they were all church leaders and religious men, highly respected in the community.

Back to the story in John 8, Jesus looked at the woman, looked at the situation, looked at the hate mongers and immediately went into big brother mode as protector; defense lawyer mode as advocate and intercessor; and news writer as reporter of the untold stories. That's just the way Jesus is. He is whatever you need Him to be for you. Do you need a big brother, a lawyer, an advocate, an intercessor or a news writer? Jesus is your man and He is your God.

He reached down to the ground but not to gather rocks. He started writing the dirty news about the woman's accusers. And soon enough, each of her accusers saw his dirt written in the dirt.

Jesus was telling them essentially: Your deeds need to line up with your creed. And so each accuser went quietly away.

Jesus loved that woman right where she was: ashamed, caught, condemned, trembling, dirty, abused, and afraid. And Jesus loved her too much to leave her where she was. That's why He told her to go *and* to sin no more. Through human tradition many receive criticism and condemnation. Through Jesus' love all may receive correction and commendation.

Jesus was telling this woman in so many words: Honey, if you confess your sins, I am faithful and just to forgive your sins, and to cleanse you from *all* unrighteousness. So just forget those things that are behind you. And reach for the things that are ahead. Don't stay where you are. Change this place for a better place. Change this lifestyle for a better, a pure lifestyle. Yesterday is gone; forget about it. Today is a new day; live it. And on the horizon is a glorious tomorrow; get to it! Get up! Go out of sin and into God's glory.

Press toward the mark of the prize of your high calling, because God indeed has a call on your life. Hear Jesus say to you: I am the Door. Leave your past with Me. I will cover your sins. I have closed the door on your past, and no man can open it. And I have opened the door to your future, and no man can shut it. This promise is recorded in Isaiah 22:22.

Move out of your past and into your future.

Move from tragedy to triumph.

Move from test to testimony.

Move from failure to fruitfulness.

Move from the bad, to better, to best.

Be all that you can be.

Do all you can do.

You can do all things through Christ who strengthens you.

Hear Him say to you: When you are feeling weak, I am strong. Don't worry. I can see that you have reached your limit, but I'm just getting started. When you come to the end of your rope, my strong arm is upholding you. I've got you. I'll hold you up. Your extremity is my opportunity. It's not by your might; you have none. It's not by your power; you have none. But it is by my Spirit, says the Lord of hosts. Look! I have forgiven you. I have covered you. I have strengthened you. I am establishing you. I am going to bless you. And I want to use you to bless others, in my name. So move forward. Make progress. Get yourself up out of here, and go-o-o-o-o!

So Jesus is telling us today through the Word of God that He came to set the record straight. The precious life and blood of Jesus Christ bring forgiveness, cleansing, healing, salvation, and restoration. The Bible says, "For God sent not his Son into the world to condemn the world, but that the world through him might be saved" (John 3:17). Please read on to verse 21.

Jesus wants us to know that He did not come to earth to condemn us. No! He came to help us and to heal us, to comfort us and to convert us, to rescue us and to restore us.

Jesus did not come to *hold* women back. He came to *pull* women back. He came here to p-u-l-l them back, like pulling back an object in a sling shot, for release into a soaring journey, an aimed and focused destination, far above and beyond that which tradition and culture have imposed on them.

Jesus came not to condemn their past.

Jesus came not to condone their past.

Jesus came to cleanse them of their past.

He came to cover their past and close the door of their past.

He came to guide them into a deep-space dimension of believing and belonging, of direction and destiny, of mentorship and of mirroring the image and likeness of eternal Holy Spirit Mother.

Christ Jesus came to release women, men, boys and girls, to set them free:

Free from the slavery of sin.

Free from the death of sin.

Free from the lies of sin.

Free from the culture and tradition caused by sin.

And they, whom the Son has set free, are free indeed, according to John 8:36.

Just use your wings and f-l-y!

Soar above your limited way of thinking.

Soar above any idea of inferiority.

Soar out of your past and into your future.

Soar into your place of divine destiny.

Jesus never went to any place by accident. All of his journeys had purpose. And Jesus never met a person, a situation, a mob, a problem, a disease, or anything that intimidated Him or that made Him anxious. Jesus never encountered people to make them feel bad about themselves. Anything that is a "put down" is not of God.

Jesus Himself, His freely flowing blood is the all-purpose, all-mighty, all-fabric-of-life, spot-removing cleanser. He can clean any of life's stains, any spill, any mess-up, any mistake, any waste, any habit, any generational iniquity, and all sin. Jesus is not in any way nervous about your condition. Your past and your present do not scare Him. He is not a respecter of sickness, addictions, behavior, circumstances, or death. He is able to handle them all.

And Jesus is very hopeful of your future. You can always get to Jesus. He is accessible. He is reachable. He is touchable. Jesus is waiting there at the point of your very need. He made sure to get there before you did. He is right there in the temple court, teaching and waiting for you. He knows you are being dragged by the mob through the streets, into the temple courts. But don't worry. Jesus will not touch that sack of rocks that the mob has dragged along. He will never hurt you. But He will surely write your accusers' dirt in the dirt if He has to.

Jesus is waiting there at the point of your very need. He made sure to get there before you did.

Need a Mirror?

Do *you* have a mob mentality? Do you convict and condemn others based on what things look like? Do you look at the situation from every angle before you form an opinion? And if you think you have indeed studied it from all angles, do you actually think your opinion counts? It does not. God has told you, "Judge not" (Matthew 7:1). So if you do judge other folks He is going to write your dirt in the dirt! Do you want your dirt written up by God? This is the counsel of Philippians 2:12, "Work out your own [your own, your own] salvation with fear and trembling." God knows that this process will take you a lifetime to accomplish. So you will not have time to mind other folks' business nor judge, condemn, convict, and execute them! Apostle Paul tells you to find your own work and do it. He says to keep busy with your own life.

You can easily identify the people who have given up on their own salvation, or who think they are perfect. They are not hard to find. They are the ones who are always in other folks' business. They are always talking about other people, telling others what they heard about somebody and giving their unsolicited opinions on that which does not concern them. In direct opposition to Matthew 28:20, these people have signed up as missionaries of information, spreading the bad news of the gossip to the ends of the church…and lo, Satan will be with them always, even to their very end. Apostle Paul has good advice for such persons. He puts it this way: "Therefore you have no excuse, O man, whoever you are, when you judge another; for in passing judgment upon him you condemn yourself, because you, the judge, are doing the very same things" (Romans 2:1 RSV).

Now do not misunderstand what I am saying. Certainly there are times when people are to correct and admonish those who are in error. Careful correction, gentle guidance and constructive criticism, as opposed to destructive criticism, should be done in the proper way and by the right people. Who are the right people? They are those who have your best interest and spiritual growth in mind when they are correcting you. And Paul even tells us that such people must make sure that their own obedience is fulfilled.

Jesus visits this issue of judging others in His sermon on the mount. Matthew 7:1-5 NIV reads: "Do not judge, or you too will be judged. For in the same way you judge others, you will be judged, and with the measure you use, it will be measured to you. Why do you look at the speck of sawdust in your brother's eye and pay no attention to the plank in your own eye? How can you say to your brother, 'Let me take the speck out of your eye,' when all the time there is a plank in your own eye? You hypocrite, first take the plank out of your own eye, and then you will see clearly to remove the speck from your brother's eye."

Additionally, we know that presenting truth to someone through the works of the flesh is not at all an effective method of correction. The truth of the Spirit must be presented in the fruit of the Spirit; otherwise, you can just "forget it," as it will definitely be ineffective.

Who is this Guy?

In Mark 8:27-29 Jesus asked His disciples, "Whom do men say that I am?" And they answered, "John the Baptist: but some say, Elias; and others, One of the prophets." Then Jesus persisted: But what about you? Who do you say I am? Peter answered, "Thou art the Christ!"

And so today, here and now, Jesus is asking each person who men say He is? I'll answer that: Well, *they* say that You are a member of a three-man family unit, called the Trinity.

He asks again: But what about you? Who do *you* say I am?

I say: Well, You are the Son of God. You are the Son of Father God, and the Son of Holy Spirit Mother God. You are a member of the perfect model family, the Holy Trinity, legitimate and authentic.

Jesus persists: Who do people say I am?

I answer: Well, they say that You are a stone thrower. They say that You condone domestic violence, public humiliation, condemnation, and devaluation of women.

He presses the issue: But how about you? Who do you say I am?

I say: You are a news writer on dirt, a big brother, a defender, an advocate, and a protector. You are the One who says that You will bless them that bless me and curse him who curses me (Genesis 12:3). You are an enemy to my enemies and an adversary to my adversaries (Exodus 23:22). You, Jesus, are the One who summons justice from the east and mercy from the west to touch me with a kiss of peace, according to Psalms 85:10.

Jesus asks again: Who do men say I am?

I say: Well they say that You are too busy for women and children, that You just can't be bothered.

He persists: But who do you say I am?

I say: Jesus, I heard You say that whoever wanted to do so could come, and whoever believes wouldn't perish, and that You'd give everyone with heavy burdens rest (Revelation 22:17, John 3:16 and Matthew 11:28).

I know who You are, Jesus!
You are not who they say You are.
You are better than that.
I know who You are, Jesus!
You are not who they try to make me believe You are.
You are more than that.
I know who You are, Jesus!

You are not who they wishfully think You are.
You are holier than that.
You are my king, and my best friend.
You are my Lord and my Savior.
You are my hero, my compassionate Hero.
You are in love with me, and I am in love with You!

Jesus, didn't you know that you're my hero?
You are all that Mary Magdalene, the woman at the well, the lady with the issue of blood, Jairus' daughter, the widow of Nain, others, and I have found You to be.
You are the updraft that takes us from the dusty roads of life and sin into the third heaven. You mount us on wings like an eagle.

You, Jesus, are the Righteous Son of God.
You are the God of Redemption.
You are the God of Relief.
You are the God of Rebirth.
You are the God of Renewal.
You are the God of Reconciliation.
You, Jesus, are the God of Reconnection.
You are the Almighty God, the God of Restoration!
You are the One who has begun a good work in me.
And You are faithful to complete it.
Hallelujah to my King!

I say to myself, to all women and to all men, don't worry and don't be afraid because Jesus Christ is waiting for you in the temple court. His love lifted me. And Jesus will lift you, because He is God and God is love. Yes, Love lifted me. Jesus lifted me out of the pit into which I had fallen, a season of depression, self-hate, low self-esteem and guilt. Jesus is reaching down to you now, and He will lift you up.

God's concern for women and men, boys and girls alike is recorded in Psalms 91:14-16: "Because they have set their love upon me, therefore will I deliver them: I will set them on high because they have known my name. They shall call upon me, and I will answer them: I will be with them in trouble; I will deliver them, and honor them. With long life will I satisfy them, and show them my salvation."

Do you want to be forgiven?

Do you want to begin again?

Do you want protection?

Do you want deliverance?

Do you want to be lifted up?

Do you want Jesus Christ to set you up?

He says: I will set them on high because they have known my name.

If you believe in His name, if you speak and call out His name, if you live in and according to His name, He promises to set you on high.

What is His name? Jesus' name is above every other name in heaven and on earth. Jesus' name is the name that meets you at your point of need.

Jesus is everything to me. He is my total supplier and dearest Friend. And He wants to be that for you.

Jesus is All I Need

When I am sick, He is the Great Physician and comes with healing in His wings.

When I am hungry, He is the Bread of Life.

When I am thirsty, He is the Living Water.

When I am in my darkest night, He is the Bright and Morning Star.

When I can't find my way, He is the Lamp unto my feet and the Light unto my path.

When I have no place to go, He is my Shelter in the time of storm.

When I am searching, He is the Way, the Truth and the Life.

When I am trying to just hold on, He is the Author and Finisher of my faith.

When I am lonely, He is the Friend that sticks closer than a brother.

When I can't see the beauty, He is the Rose of Sharon, the Lily of the Valley. He is altogether lovely.

When I need tender care, He is the Good Shepherd.

When I suffer loss, He sends my Comforter.

When I am in sinking sand, He is the solid rock.

When I am experiencing an identity crisis, He is the Root and Offspring of David, the Son of God, and the Son of Mary.

When I am in a state of confusion and turmoil, He is Jehovah Shalom, the Prince of Peace.

When I don't know where to start or where to stop, He is Alpha and Omega, the beginning and the end, the first and the last.

When I am being bullied and need strong back up, He is the Lion of Judah, the Mighty Conqueror.

When I am marching into battle, He is my helmet of salvation and my breastplate of righteousness.

When I can't seem to get off the ground, He is the wind beneath my wings.

When I have no one to love and no one to love me, God is Love. And He whose name is Jealous loves me.

When I am in need of family, He is my elder Brother.

When the future is in quandary, He is the ecclesiastical expectation, the Hope of Glory.

When I am exposed in shame, He is the robe of righteousness.

When I stand accused, He is the defender of the brethren.

When my case seems hopeless, He is the Righteous Judge and full of mercy.

When I am guilty as charged, He is the great sacrifice.

When I am stained with sin, He is the fountain filled with blood.

When I need to get to the Father, His name gives me access.

When the darkness of this earth presses in, He is the Light of the world.

When it feels like I am locked out, He is the gate that opens to life eternal.

When it seems like I'm about to drown, He walks on water and with His mighty hand He lifts me up. He can even part the sea.

When I am in broken relationships, He is the repairer of the breach.

When I can't figure out who is who, He is King, according to Saint Matthew; Servant, according to Saint Mark; man according to Saint Luke; and God according to Saint John.

He is Immanuel, El Shaddai, Elohim, Ebenezer, Adonai, Yahweh, Jehovah Jirah, Jehovah Raphe, Jehovah Nissi, Jehovah Tsidkenu and He is Jehovah M'Kaddesh.

When I can feel the shadow of death, He is the Risen Savior.

When I come to the end of my life, He is life eternal.

When I am in any kind of need, "I will lift up mine eyes unto the hills from whence cometh my help. My help cometh from the Lord, who made the heavens and the earth" (Psalms 121:1, 2).

Chapter Seven

Family of Women Winners

And so, dear readers, you must understand who women are and how important they are in the eyes of God. It's all in the Word of God. That's why we have been admonished to "study to show thyself approved unto God…rightly dividing the word of truth" (2 Timothy 2:15). So study God's word for yourself. You will find that God has His stamp of approval on women. You don't have to believe what they tell you in school. You don't have to listen to what they say in the workplace. You don't have to believe the misconstrued views of your grandparents or your parents. Just believe and live by what the Lord says concerning who women are. And it's all been demonstrated in Jesus' life, the Word of God made flesh.

Jesus seals His bride with the Holy Spirit. And it is the Holy Spirit who adorns the bride for the groom. Holy Spirit Mother takes the bride and teaches her, guides her, stays with her, empowers her, comforts her, hovers over her to protect her, influences her, nurtures and develops her into becoming gloriously presentable, without spot or wrinkle or any such thing, but that she should be holy and without blemish (Ephesians 5:27). And just as a woman anointed and prepared Jesus for His burial, a woman, His bride prepares for His return.

2 Corinthians 3:18. "But we all, with open face beholding as in a glass the glory of the Lord, are changed into the same image from glory to glory, even as by the Spirit of the Lord."

Let's look at this text for what it means in the body of Christ as well as a revelation of the personality of the Holy Spirit. To whom does a woman go for council and for a better understanding of the man she is about to marry? To whom does the married woman go in order to further learn of the one whom she has married? The wise woman goes to the man's mother to learn all about her lover. She hopefully has figured out that this source of experiential knowledge and understanding can only come by way of the man's mother. And as the woman beholds him through the "words of witness" of his mother, she can have a deeper understanding and open communion with him. His mother has revealed so many things about her son to his wife, that she, her daughter-in-law can actually know him on a level otherwise unable to be known without that mother's insight and revelation. And so by this association with the man's mother, the woman will become a part of him (two shall become one) in an even more meaningful way.

In much the same way, beholding—learning about, interacting with—Christ, we become changed into His likeness, purpose and spirit. The bride as the church, is the body of Christ. And it is through the witness of Holy Spirit Mother that we learn more and understand better, the Person of Jesus Christ as Head and Bridegroom of the Church.

Revelation 22:19. "And the Spirit and the bride say, Come. And let him that heareth say, Come. And let him that is athirst come. And whosoever will, let him take the water of life freely."

This verse parallels what a bride-to-be and a mother do in wedding and celebration preparations. It is mainly the role of women to send out invitations for the wedding. The invitations are used to say, "Come." And throughout the history of the post-Edenic world, the believers, the bride-church have sent the message of hope with this invitation, "Come."

So these adorning, developing, nurturing, and preparation activities are Woman-to-woman interactions. It is the Eternal Mother in the holy family of God, preparing the young bride for the wedding supper of the Lamb, where she will be joined to her groom, Jesus Christ. And there she will forever "be with the Lord" (1 Thessalonians 4:17).

So when you meet up with folks who treat women or refer to women as second best, second class, second saved, of little count, irrelevant and unimportant—the way people did thousands of years ago, and yes, some unfortunate souls still do it today. You can just look at those persons with holy pity and pray for them. Women, also open your mouth, and "Let the redeemed of the Lord say so." Tell them just who you are. Tell them that you don't *think* you are but that you *know* who you are. Men, tell them that women are the crowning creation of the Most High God.

Readers, tell them that women are friends of Jesus, and He is a friend of women. Tell them that Jesus has been close to women and has depended on women throughout the history of the world, as far back as Adam-woman in Eden. Tell them that He has used women's work. He has worked with women to accomplish His miracles. Tell them that God used feminine endowments to connect the Holy Family with the earthly family, and to bring eternal salvation to "whosoever believeth" (John 3:16). Tell them that He has counted on women for love, affection, adoration and admiration. Tell them that He has marveled at the faith of women. Tell them that women were an important part of His life and ministry, while He was here on earth, just as men were.

Tell them that Jesus pays special attention to women today. Tell them that He walks with women, and talks with women, and tells them that they are His own. Tell them that He hears and answers women's prayers. He dries their tears, mends their broken heart, heals their diseases, forgives their sins and has made them the "righteousness of God" (2 Corinthians 5:21). Tell them that as King of kings, and as Lord of lords, He is coming back soon on His white horse to gather up His bride unto Himself that where He is, women and men may be also.

Men and women of the Word, brothers and sisters of salvation, friends of the Gospel, and children of Deity must make sure that the place of women here on earth, in the family, in the church, at work, in school and in society as a whole, counts for what it was meant to be. We must support women so that their lives resemble, reflect, and represent their position in the triune family of God. Only then can they participate in life as a "true shadow of heaven" right here on earth.

Women must make sure that their influence: comforting, exhorting, edifying, audible words, motives and attitudes reflect the ministry of Holy Spirit Mother. Women have a model, a heavenly mother to pattern their life. Women have their place and position in this universe. They must take their place, do their part, be counted and make a difference in this world.

But until Jesus returns to swoop women off their feet and take them to their mansions on high, they must be assured that as followers of Christ they will be confronted by the enemy of souls. That ole sly fox, the Devil, will put people and problems in their path to discourage, distract and defeat them.

Gender Prejudice

James 2:9. "But if ye have respect to persons, ye commit sin, and are convinced of the law as transgressors." Those who show preference for race, gender, or any other endowment are not abiding in God's Law.

Galatians 3:28. "There is neither Jew nor Greek, there is neither bond nor free, *there is neither male nor female*: for ye are all one in Christ Jesus." There should be no distinctions, no inequality between genders in the church, in Christ. For too long we have been taught that man is the head of the woman. This is not biblical. The Bible says that the husband is the head of *the* wife—*his own wife.*

Women must make sure that their influence: comforting, exhorting, edifying, audible words, motives and attitudes reflect the ministry of Holy Spirit Mother. Women have a model, a heavenly mother to pattern their life. Women have their place and position in this universe. They must take their place, do their part, be counted and make a difference in this world.

These are two completely different concepts. So as it relates to life and life in the church and out of the church, a man has the responsibility of partner-provider-servant (Mark 9:35) to a woman only *if* that woman is his wife. A man does not have partner-provider responsibility to *any and all women—just to his own wife.* This is why the Bible says, "wives submit to *your own* husband," as opposed to being submitted to any other man. The understanding of submission will be covered later in this book.

Gender problems should not exist in the church. If the problem does exist anywhere, it should only exist within the individual family where husband and wife must work it out according to the Word of God. Therefore, the attitude we see prevalent in many church organizations today is not biblical. Unless we have the attitude of Jesus Christ concerning women, we will not see Him in peace.

1 Corinthians 3:16, 17 The Living Bible (TLB). "Don't you realize *that all of you together,* are the house, and that the Spirit of God lives among you in His house? If anyone defiles and spoils God's home, God will destroy him. For God's home is holy and clean, and *you are that home.*" Christ, and not man, is the head of His home, the Church. So if man defiles the house of God with teachings and practices not backed by God's Word, God will destroy him. In 1 Corinthians 2:13,14 (NIV) we read, "This is what we speak, not in words taught us by human wisdom but in words taught by the Spirit, expressing spiritual truths in spiritual words. The man without the Spirit does not accept the things that come from the Spirit of God, for they are foolishness to him, and he cannot understand them, because they are spiritually discerned."

Ephesians 2:21, 22, TLB. Apostle Paul tells the church, "We who believe are joined together with Christ as parts of a beautiful, constantly growing temple for God. And you also are joined with him and with each other by the Spirit, and are part of this dwelling place of God."

Galatians 5:25. "If we live in the Spirit, let us also walk in the Spirit." We should not profess to be spiritual people while living according to sinful traditions of the flesh.

Ephesians 4:2 and 2 Timothy 1:7. "Make every effort to keep the unity of the Spirit through the bond of peace." Where there is inequity, there is no peace. There may be toleration, but certainly not peace (Galatians 4: 29). Sometimes certain tolerances are caused by fear, fear of change, and fear of the sacrifice required to effect change. But to this, the Bible speaks as well, "For God has not given us the spirit of fear; but of power, and of love, and of a sound mind." The time is at hand for all believers of God's truth to take a stand for the right. Sin has to be called by its right name. And courageous love in action is the way to pull down the strongholds of sinful tradition in religious institutions and in society.

Romans 16:1, 2. "I commend unto you Phoebe our sister, which is a servant of the church, which is at Cenchrea: that ye receive her in the Lord, as becometh saints, and that ye assist her in whatsoever business she hath need of you: for she hath been a succourer of many, and of myself also." Phoebe is a woman who had worked with Apostle Paul. She was coming to Rome to share and work her ministries there. *Assist* more closely resembles the word *submit* in Greek. This submission would not have been a problem in the body of Christ. Ephesians 5:21: "Submit yourselves one to another in the fear of God."

Romans 16: 3, 4. "Greet Priscilla and Aquila my helpers in Christ Jesus: Who have for my life laid down their own necks: unto whom not only I give thanks, but also all the churches of the Gentiles." Paul commends and greets Priscilla and her husband, Aquila, in the sequence not culturally correct in that place and time. So why would he do it this way? Because the Church is the body of Christ where there is neither male nor female. That is why. And perhaps Priscilla was the more active person in helping Paul's ministry. She would have had more time to help, since the men were working, providing for the family as they are supposed to do. Perhaps she was a well-spoken person who gave Bible lesson studies publicly and was more widely known.

It seems as though Apostle Paul is more progressive than some people I have come across in the ministry God has developed through me. My husband, Maurice, works to take care of his family. I have been in laity ministry long before I was married, and it has progressed to this present level. There certainly have been some people who try to make sure that my husband gets the comments and credits for the ministry, which he did not establish nor carries. Maurice of course immediately corrects such insinuations and well understands their intentions.

At one church where my young children have been active in their public speaking ministry, a church officer talked with Maurice and me together asking which one of us writes the speeches and teaches them to the children. My husband told him that his children's mother does these things. This man seemed to be disappointed that I, a woman, was responsible for our children's ministry. Then soon after our returning to this church from ministering out of town, this official held the door of the church opened as my children and I walked toward it. The children entered the door, greeting and thanking him. As I started to enter, he closed the door in my face and while holding the glass door shut, he said, "Now that we have the children, we can do without the mother." So I can tell you that there is indeed a real problem that needs purging by the Holy

Spirit. But I have not given up nor given in. I just keep pressing forward, continuing in the assignment God has given me.

So when women hold on, hang in there, remembering who they are and whose they are, they will be victorious Christians. The Bible says that when the enemy rushes in like a flood, the Spirit of the Lord will raise up a standard, a banner of victory against him. The Holy Spirt is Jehovah Nissi, our victory in battle. No matter how women are treated, they must stand firm and know that what was meant for evil, God will surely turn it for their good. So just persevere.

Out of your mess will come a message.

Out of your tragedy will come triumph.

Out of your test will come testimony.

Out of your brokenness will come blessing.

Out of your burden will come benefit.

Out of your sorrow will come serenity.

Out of your pain will come power.

The world around you may be in utter shambles, but your joy remains. "Though the earth be removed, though the mountains be carried into the midst of the sea, though the waters roar and be troubled, though the mountains shake with the swelling thereof" (Psalms 46:2, 3, 5) your joy remains. Psalms 47:1, 2 says "Clap your hands, all you nations; shout to God with cries of JOY. How awesome is the Lord God Most High, the great King over all the earth!"

He will put you on the top and never on the bottom. Jesus is the power you need, to get you, where you need to be.

He will put you at the head and not at the tail.

He will put you in the front and not in the back.

Jesus is King of kings and Lord of lords.

Jesus is your knight in shining armor.

Ride on King Jesus. No man, and no psyched-out woman, can hinder me. Ride on, King Jesus. Ride on. No man, no woman, no demon force, no devil in hell, nothing in the air, nothing on the earth, nothing in the waters under the earth, no mountain, no door, no storm, no circumstance, no situation, nothing, not anything, can hinder me. Ride on, ride on, King Jesus! Glory to God Almighty.

Jesus had deliberate, up close and personal interaction with women during His time on earth. God ordained this relationship, because He was trying to tell us something. God is telling us that women and men are to be equally valued, loved, accepted and celebrated.

Jesus was developed into fetal maturity inside a woman. The first flesh He touched on this earth was that of a woman. The first eyes He looked into were those of a woman.

Satan's Lies

- **Women are less than God's best.**
- **Wife and mother are not worthy callings.**
- **Women should not be in leadership, because the Bible speaks against it.**
- **Women's services that help to build up the church and plant seed in God's kingdom and into the community are not noteworthy.**
- **Women who take their God-appointed place are a problem.**

One of the first persons in the Temple to recognize baby Jesus as the Christ, the incarnate Son of God, was Prophetess Anna. And she was the first person to spread the news of his identity.

A woman, Mother Mary, taught Jesus who He is and who His Father is, as well as lessons of life and of eternity.

A woman, Jesus' mother, was the first person to make a demand on His anointing by having Him turn water into wine.

The first person to take Jesus' healing ministry public was a woman, Peter's Mother-in-law, after He healed her of a fever.

The first person to whom Jesus called himself Messiah was a woman, the woman at the well. Then she evangelized an entire city, taking Jesus' ministry to another level.

A woman was one of Jesus' best friends. Mary Magdalene was the most forthright in demonstrating her deep love and affection, admiration and adoration.

Mary Magdalene anointed Jesus for His burial. She was the only disciple who understood the deeper truth of the physical death her Lord was to soon enter. When the men condemned her actions, Jesus immediately rebuked them (Mark 14:3-8 and Luke 7:37-50).

A lad's mother prepared a lunch of fish and bread that Jesus used to feed thousands of men and women, boys and girls at one meal.

The documented miracles of raising people from the dead were performed, for the most part, at the request of or on behalf of women.

Jesus commended a Canaanite woman for her great faith (Matthew 15:28).

Only Pilate's wife confronted him about the plan to crucify Jesus (Matthew 27:17-19).

Women openly wept for Jesus as He carried the cross up Golgotha's hill (Luke 23:27).

Women were the ones most faithful in following Jesus to Calvary. The male disciples, except for young John, forsook Jesus and fled.

As Conqueror over death and hell Jesus first appeared to Mary in peace, and called her by name (John 20:13-16).

Jesus appeared to His women disciples on three different occasions after His resurrection before appearing to the men.

Jesus sent women—not Peter, not John—but women to tell the disciples that He had risen (John 20:15-18; Matthew 28:1-10; Mark 16:1-11, Luke 24:1-12).

Just before giving up His spirit while hanging on the cross, Jesus made life-care arrangements for a woman, His own mother, Mary.

Jesus calls His people, His Church, "the bride, the Lamb's wife" (Revelation 21:2, 9) and does not use masculine terms to describe His Church.

Chapter Eight

Family Daughters

Hear this because the same holds true for you: God has the provision for the vision He placed in my spirit. So I meditate on it, and my tongue speaks of it continually. Because according to Proverbs 18:21, "Life and death are in the power of the tongue." The power of life and death are in the words I choose to speak over my life. God has also said in Deuteronomy 30:19, "I have set before you life and death, blessing and cursing: therefore choose life, that both thou and thy seed may live."

Choose to speak empowerment.
Choose to speak progress.
Choose to speak prosperity.
Choose to speak profit.
Choose to speak positivity.
Choose to speak peace.

Choose to speak victory so that it may go well with you and also with your children. According to Proverbs 12:14, what you *speak* over your life is just as important as what you *do* to obtain the kind of life you desire.

So when haters hurt you and you have a chance for revenge, choose life. "Blessed are you when people insult you, persecute you and falsely say all kinds of evil against you…because great is your reward in heaven" (Matthew 5:11, 12 NIV).

When things get tough and you want to quit, choose life. "But he who stands firm to the end will be saved" (Mark 13:13 NIV).

When your situation calls for sadness and depression, choose life. "The joy of the Lord is your strength" (Nehemiah 8:10).

When that thing feels good to you but it is not good for you, choose life. "There is a way that seems right… but in the end it leads to death" (Proverbs 16:25 NIV).

When after you've decided to follow Jesus, the world pulls at you, choose life. "And be not conformed to this world: but be ye transformed by the renewing of your mind, that ye may prove what is that good, and acceptable, and perfect, will of God" (Romans 12:2).

When it is easier for you to be put in a gender box by others, choose life. As previously noted, "There is neither...male nor female; for ye are all one in Christ Jesus" (Galatians 3:28).

You are commanded to provide a legacy and a heritage for your children and for generations following you, because you are an heir according to the promise (Genesis 12:2, 3; Galatians 3:29).

The Holy Spirit of the living God empowers me to speak God's word of truth over my life. And the sword of the Spirit is always victorious over the attacks and lies of tradition the enemy forms against me. You see, I am able to speak the truth over my life because I know what the truth is. If I didn't know it, I would not be able to speak it. The enemy wants to blind our mind to the truth of God's Word. Because if you don't know the truth, you can't claim that truth for yourself, so there will be no power in that word for you. You have not made it yours. This is ignorance, a lack of knowledge of God's word.

Satan's only real weapon against you is the weapon of ignorance. He has destroyed many dreams and many lives through ignorance. Ignorance comes from laziness, lack of effort to search out the truth. Ignorance is complacent satisfaction with taking someone else's interpretation of truth without your studying it also. Ignorance is also the rejection of truth. God's Word tells us that the end result of ignorance is destruction. He says, "My people are destroyed for the lack of knowledge: because they have rejected knowledge, I will also reject thee" (Hosea 4:6). God's word also tells us of the rewards of getting the knowledge of truth. His Word says, "Grace and peace be multiplied unto you through the knowledge… of the gospel" (2 Peter 1:2). So we see that grace and peace, power and prosperity are bountiful when God's truth, as it is in Jesus, is known and applied accurately. Accurate application of His Word to your own life and situations is wisdom. We are to be wise unto salvation. Salvation speaks not only of eternal life, but also of abundant life here and now. Salvation also speaks of the removal of oppression and anything that keeps you from reaching your full potential as one created in the image of God.

Promises Address Problems

In Revelation 12:11, we find that those who are conquerors are those who have victory in life. They know and do the right combination of things: "They overcame by the blood of the Lamb and by the word of their testimony." *So the truth of Jesus and speaking that truth over your own life is the winning combination.*

The psalmist understood this powerful combination as well. Psalms 71:15, 16 and 24: "But I will hope continually [in God], and will yet praise thee more and more. My mouth shall show forth thy righteousness and thy salvation all the day; …I will go in the strength of the Lord God: I will make mention of thy righteousness, even of thine only…. My tongue also shall talk of thy righteousness all the day long: for they are confounded, for they are brought to shame, that seek my hurt." He understood the key to overcoming spiritual and earthly enemies and living a life of victory.

The more you are chased by evil and by evil people, the faster you must run into the presence of God for safety. We already know how to get into God's presence, right? We get into the throne room of the Lord by entering into His gates and through His courts with singing, praise, and thanksgiving. Praise gets you raised. These activities of worship will escort you into the Holy of Holies. It is there that you will find your seat next to Christ. The Bible says, God has "raised us up with Christ and seated us with him in the heavenly realms in Christ Jesus" (Ephesians 2:6 NIV). And while you are there sitting in His presence, you are safe. This sitting position gives God permission to lift up a banner of victory against your enemies. This is the time that God can legitimately say, "The battle is not yours, it's the Lords." The Spirit of the Lord is your Jehovah *Nissi.*

The next time you are troubled, remember that your words can bail you out, build you up, or take you down. It's your choice. Speak the promises instead of the problems. Speak in faith and not from feelings. Speak of Christ and not of circumstances. Try it!

So I commission you wonderful readers of the Word, readers of Truth:

Be pregnant with life.

Be pregnant with hope.

Be expectant with the ever-living seed of the Word of God.

God says that He has thoughts of goodwill toward you, plans to prosper you, plans to give you hope and a future. Your future is found in the Word of God. Speak the Word over your future, because your future is in the power of your tongue. Call "those things which be not as though they were" so that they will come forth (see Isaiah 46:10 and Romans 4:17).

The next time you are troubled, remember that your words can bail you out, build you up, or take you down. It's your choice. Speak the promises instead of the problems. Speak in faith and not from feelings. Speak of Christ and not of circumstances. Try it!

Realize that doubt delays destiny but focused faith flourishes to fruition. The best is yet to come! Do not live in doubt. Just focus your faith on the promises of God. They are all right there, in the Bible. God is bigger than your circumstances.

Women are pregnant with positivism and pinnacle expectation. Their water just broke. It is time. Women are ready to birth a new day, a brighter day, a day of victory for themselves and for those in the sphere of their influence. It may be painful at times, but delivery is inevitable. "Lift up your heads; for your redemption draweth nigh" (Luke 21:28).

And women must be careful not to injure that precious new life they are bringing forth. No negative speaking, gossiping (Psalms 15:3), murmuring, and things that God abhors. They must not loose their focus of God's ideal for them, by accepting as doctrine, the commandments and traditions of men (Mark 7:8). They must not be afraid to call sin by its name.

Realize that doubt delays destiny but focused faith flourishes to fruition. The best is yet to come!

Colossians 2:8-10 and 15: "Beware lest any man spoil you through philosophy and vain deceit, after the tradition of men, after the rudiments of the world, and not after Christ. For in Him dwelleth all the fullness of the Godhead bodily. And ye are complete in Him, which is the head of all principality and power.... And having spoiled principalities and powers, He made a show of them openly, triumphing over them in it." So we can see here that just as a child contains genetic material of both his father and mother, so in Jesus dwells the fullness of the Godhead in his body, sharing deity with Father God, and Holy Spirit Mother. When we embrace this truth and live by it, we too will ruin the principalities and powers of darkness "in this present world."

Women must go ahead and pant with focus. Push. Push out that promising life so that you can see it, hold it, nurture it, and enjoy it.

Will You Accept Your Assignment?

Again, let me remind women to choose the life that comes out of God's mouth about who they are. Forget about what comes out of tradition-speaking mouths. Because God is always right. And women are created in God's image, in the image of Holy Spirit Mother! She is the God of abundance, the breasted God who has the provision for each vision. Because of Jesus Christ, our elder Brother, we have received the promised Holy Spirit. Jesus is the Hope of glory, according to Colossians 1:27. He came to bring us hope and a glorious future. By accepting the person and principles of Jesus Christ, we become "a chosen people, a royal priesthood, a holy nation, a people belonging to God" and can live our life in total victory. Please read 1 Peter 2:9 (NIV).

Your assignment for life is found in God's Word, the only truth. God has no hidden agenda, no ulterior motive, and no sin in His heart. "God is not a man that He should lie, nor the son of man that He should change His mind" (Numbers 23:19). So then, that makes you bigger than people's reassignment for you. That makes you better than people's dream for you. That makes you braver than people's intimidations aimed at you. For higher than the highest, humanly thoughts, dreams, goals and desires can imagine is God's plan for His children. And you are indeed a child of God through Jesus Christ. You have a good reason to shout right about now!

I am certainly not in rebellion. No indeed. I just refuse to be reassigned. I already have my assignment from the God family. God has assigned my value. He has assigned my role. And He has assigned to me a heavenly role model. Her name is Spirit of God,

Holy Spirit Mother, Spirit of promise and Spirit of truth. She is my model because She is my heavenly Mother God. So I do not need to be in rebellion. I just need to follow the heavenly plan. Indeed this is not a sinful rebellion; this is a spiritual renaissance, a saving resolution. And I will not relent, relinquish nor rest until I get what is rightfully mine. All that encompasses my life is a done deal, an undisputable fact, a biblical reality. It was all taken care of, ordained and recorded in Genesis. God's plan is recorded in Genesis 1:26-28: Let "us" make humankind in "our" image and after "our" likeness. And God did just that: Created "male and female" and blessed "them." God gave both of them dominion over the earth (Genesis 1:26-28). Any other teaching is a lie from the pit of hell.

You see, those whom God created in His own image and likeness are the ones to whom He also gave dominion over the earth. This is why it is important to point out that the female was given dominion equal to that given to the male, according to the Bible. God put them both in charge of the earth. Only after sin entered did God charge the husband with the responsibility of providing for his family under adverse conditions, as a partner-provider. This has *nothing* to do with the image, likeness and dominion of both male and female. And it has nothing to do with the status of equality of the husband and wife within the family structure.

Additionally, we know that all males are not married. And certainly, all females are not married. As stated earlier, if a woman is led to believe that only the male was made in God's image and likeness, then she will also understandably buy into the notion that only the male was given dominion, and that whatever the she gets has to come to her from the male. This is certainly not scriptural. Adam-female-woman was renamed "Eve" by a sinful man. She should have refused that name and retained the name God had given her. Her name was Adam just like her husband.

In Genesis 17:15 we see that God the Creator changed the name of Sarai to Sar*ah* just as He changed the name of Abram to Abr*ah*am. Their names were changed by God to reflect the name Y*ah*weh. This change of name reflected God's image, likeness, and covenant relationship with each of them, individually, as male and as female. God separately gave Sarah her own dominion by announcing that He would bless her and make her a mother of nations. God made sure that Sarah understood the fact that she had her own dominion, her own name, and her own legacy. This is God's ideal for all women today. You must know the truth. The truth will set you free.

And now let us take a look at Proverbs 31:10-31. Let us look at one such woman, the virtuous woman, with a deeper insight than we have in the past:

"Who can find a virtuous woman? For her price is far above rubies. The heart of her husband doth safely trust in her, so that he shall have no need of spoil. She will do him good and not evil all the days of her life. She seeketh wool, and flax and worketh willingly with her hands. She is like the merchants' ships; she bringeth her food from afar. She riseth also while it is yet night, and giveth meat to her household, and a portion to her maidens. She considereth a field, and buyeth it; with the fruit of her hands she planteth a vine-yard. She girdeth her loins with strength, and strengtheneth her arms. She perceiveth that her merchandise is good; her candle goeth not out by night. She layeth her hands to the spindle, and her hands hold the distaff. She stretcheth out her hand to the poor; yea, she reacheth forth her hands to the needy. She is not afraid of the snow for her household; for all her household are clothed with scarlet. She maketh herself coverings of tapestry; her clothing is silk and purple. Her husband is known in the gates, when he sitteth among the elders of the land. She maketh fine linen, and selleth it; and delivereth girdles unto the merchant. Strength and honour are her clothing; and she shall rejoice in time to come. She openeth her mouth with wisdom; and in her tongue is the law of kindness. She looketh well to the ways of her household, and eateth not the bread of idleness. Her children arise up, and call her blessed; her husband also, and he praiseth her. Many daughters have done virtuously, but thou excellest them all. Favour is deceitful, and beauty is vain; but a woman that feareth the Lord, she is to be praised. Give her of the fruit of her hands; and let her own works praise her in the gates."

Hallelujah. What a woman. According to quotes from King Lemuel, King Solomon outlines attributes and activities of the ideal woman:

This kind of woman may be hard to find, perhaps due to the fact that most women see their value and limitations through the eyes of men. This woman does not. She knows who she is and knows that her value cannot be assigned her by tradition.

The husband of this woman has faith in her as an individual and understands her right of freedom and dominion, therefore trusts her.

She is her husband's counterpart, completer of the unit. So she does her part in carrying out their family mission statement all the days of her life. And what a wonderful life she has made for them both.

She is a woman not afraid of work and actually loves to work hard. She is not idle or lazy.

She is a good gatherer for her family, a smart shopper and deals fairly with her employees, which means that she is an employer.

She rises early and prepares enough food for her family and her workers.

She looks for other business opportunities outside of the home. And with her capital, she invests and works her new "field" of business to create a profit.

She takes care of her physical body so that she can stay strong and healthy to continue her responsibilities with excellence. She exercises her authority in the work that she does. And she moves in the power of the Holy Spirit.

She is also involved in community outreach affairs and generously helps the poor and the suffering. She is compassionate and not selfish. She looks over her acquisitions and goes over the books of her transactions. She oversees the quality review of her own business.

She plans well in advance for the needs and supplies of her family. The coming winter months do not make her anxious because she has already prepared.

She wears quality and dignified clothing as it speaks well of a woman in her standing.

She married well. She married a hardworking man, who is also a successful person. In fact he is a leader in the community, sitting in the office of the city and among the leaders, officials, and counselors. Her husband is accomplished, respected, and therefore, is not threatened by his wife's success.

She is a crafty, skilled, learned and industrious woman who distributes her products to merchants on ships to be sold in other ports. So we can see that she has good business rapport in her community.

She has built a strong image and reputation for herself and wears them as garments of distinction. She rejoices in her future retirement because she will not suffer lack. She is preparing for life ahead.

Her words reflect her character. She is kind and wise.

She takes good care of her family and does not buy into the notion that all she receives has to come from her husband. She has her own life and authority.

She well understands that, in order to go far in life, favor from men and physical beauty dictated by men do not form a solid foundation for her future and self- worth. She knows that her worth comes from respecting, believing, and obeying God's Holy Word. She is a woman who lives her life God's way. She is a woman worthy of praise.

Just look at this woman! And look at the kind of fulfilling life she has. She is experiencing abundant life indeed. And look at her beautiful family. They appreciate her and bless her for who she is and for what she does for them. Look at her husband. He is so happy for her. He is so blessed by the works of her hands and gives her praise both at home and in the town square. What a man, a godly man, a secure man. She is also obviously a smart woman to marry this kind of man. He is not the kind of man who would keep her from fully developing herself and expressing herself as an individual. He also does not try to take credit for the work that his wife is doing. He is just genuinely happy for her.

Chapter Nine

Family Fallacies and Forgiveness

Contrast the wonderful and virtuous husband in the Proverbs 31 family with the husband in some homes and in some traditional settings today. I recently heard a preacher expound on the story found in Judges 4 and 5. This is a story of a wife and judge in Israel named Deborah. During this time in Israel, judges were national leaders. Israel did not have a king at the time.

There was a fearful, intimidated Israelite army general named Barak. He refused to do battle against the enemy, even after God told him to do so. He then agreed to do battle only if Judge Deborah would fight alongside him. She agreed. But God told Barak that since he demanded that a woman war along side of him, then God would have a woman actually win the battle. General Barak was alright with this arrangement. Israel's army battled well and won.

A brave Kenite woman by the name of Jael, actually killed the commander of the opposing Canaanite army. King Jabin's army commander, Sisera came to her home to take a rest during the battle; and while he was asleep, she drove a stake through his skull. The people of Israel had a large victory celebration. All were invited to witness this national celebration of victory. Both women, Deborah and Jael, received proper recognition with no problem, no hesitation, without envy, without cover-up, without slight, without issue. This was the will of the Lord for these brave women.

But in the New Testament, Hebrews 11, Deborah's name is not listed as one of the faithful. Barak's name is mentioned instead. The minister's explanation was that God knew that Deborah could handle being omitted, since she is a woman. He went on to say that godly women should not desire or feel a need to be recognized for their work or accomplishments. He suggested that their focus should be on their husbands or male counterpart; and when the male receives credit for the things he accomplishes and for what the female accomplishes, that is acceptable. What a tragic teaching. What a misrepresentation of the Scriptures. What a deliberate lie. He must have forgotten to compare text with text. He forgot what was recorded by the wisest man on earth, in Proverbs 31 about the virtuous woman with her accomplishments. And he must have forgotten that Deborah's story is indeed recorded for her recognition in the Old Testament. He must have overlooked the fact that the book of Hebrews is in the New Testament, and that centuries had elapsed between the two records. So Deborah would not be aware of any omission since she was long dead when Hebrews was written. Therefore, it is not known how she would react or feel about this traditional kind of slight and oversight against women.

If this preacher's suggestions are right, then it was wrong for Deborah and Jael to participate in their own victory celebration. Accordingly, only Barak should have been honored at that grand event. So why did Deborah and Jael not go back home after they won the battle and sit in a corner in the "godly woman" stereotype and let all credit go to Barak?

And what about the texts that say laborers are worthy of their wages, and to give recognition and respect to whom it is due (Luke 10:7; Proverbs 3:27)? Are these texts only for men? God does not contradict Himself. People contradict God. We must be very careful not to customize the Word of God to our own perversion! God's Word is it's own expositor; His Word reflects His character. When anyone misrepresents His Word, it is the same as implying that God is not right, and therefore needs to be modified. This is the same as putting one's own imagination above God. This is the very essence of satanism. That is exactly why the Bible says in 1 Samuel 15:23, that the spirit of pride, which is stubbornness and tradition outside of truth, is as the spirit of witchcraft. Teaching for doctrine the traditions of men is dangerous. "Let God be true, but every man a liar" (Romans 3:4). I choose to believe and to operate in God's truth, because He is always the only Truth. And therefore, I write the wrongs to right the wrongs.

God does not contradict Himself. People contradict God.

Second Corinthians 10:5, 6 says that we are to "cast down imaginations, and every high thing that exalteth itself against the knowledge of God, and bring into captivity every thought to the obedience of Christ." We are to be ready to revenge, to correct, all disobedience when our own obedience is fulfilled. Then Apostle Paul goes on to ask, in so many words: Do you base your opinion and attitude on the outward appearance [gender or race]? If you trust that you are in Christ, remember that so are the ones against whom you discriminate (2 Corinthians 10:7).

And while we are here, let us look at a couple of related issues. It is interesting to me that in Hebrews chapter 11, only two women are named: Sarah and Rahab. I certainly can think of quite a few worthy women who could have been listed here among the faithful, such as Abigail, or even the Shunamite woman. What about Queen Esther who saved her entire nation from genocide? And what about the five daughters of the tribe of Manasseh?

Abigail went *against* her evil husband to help David, and was greatly blessed. The Shunamite woman *bypassed* her husband and sent for the prophet to raise her son from the dead. Perhaps her husband did not have enough faith to think the prophet could help his son and would have forfeited the life of his child. The five daughters of Manasseh spoke up for themselves against the system of gender discrimination.

Of these women, Sarah is the only one documented to have obeyed her husband, who was in error. Abraham sent Sarah to King Abimelech's palace fully knowing that eventually his wife would have to have sexual intercourse with this man. Abraham planned this charade out of fear, not faith. But God in His mercy visited this king in a dream and commanded him not to touch Sarah. This fascinating story is found in Genesis 20.

No one knows who wrote the book of Hebrews. We know only that it was written somewhere between A.D. 64 and A.D. 68. Peter may have influenced the author. And Apostle Peter is the same person who discriminated against the Gentiles. He felt that the gospel and the work of the gospel were only for the Jews, even after Jesus commanded them to take the gospel to all nations of the world. God corrected Peter and led him to the truth of the matter, salvation for all people, through a dream and a divine appointment with

Cornelius, a Gentile. But even after this correction, Peter continued in his prejudicial posturing. Because we find that Paul had to confront him later on this same issue. Peter and Paul parted company because of this issue. See Galatians chapter two.

I have often wondered why Jesus asked Peter three times in one conversation, "Do you love me?" After Peter's reply, Jesus then said to him, "Feed my sheep." What does this mean? I believe that Jesus was addressing Peter's three-fold prejudices. One question addresses Peter's prejudice against women. The second addresses his intolerance of the little children (Luke 18:15, 16); and the last, his attitude toward Gentiles. All are sheep of the Good Shepherd, Jesus Christ. Jesus was simply trying to lead Peter into a wider dimension of ministry and tolerance. Please read John 21:15-17.

Peter and the other disciples indeed discriminated against women. Review the story Matthew 15:22-29. And review the story of Acts 1:21-26, where Peter overlooked Mary and the other female disciples for nomination into apostleship. Instead, he nominated two men, Matthias and Justus, as "election" choices. We hear nothing about either of these men after the vote took place. Perhaps it is because they did nothing noteworthy for the early church. It reminds me of some churches today, where there are elected men who, as self-promoters, do very little for the body of Christ, yet hold the title and the seat of authority, while the women of the same organization work tirelessly yet never make it into such positions of authority and honor. This is a generational religious iniquity.

Mary and the other women were disciples of Jesus. But more than that, Jesus had personally chosen Mary and the other women to witness His resurrection first, and sent them to tell the male disciples, "He is alive!" So you can easily see that any of these women qualified to be voted in as an "elected" apostle. The men did not even believe these women's eyewitness account concerning the risen Savior; and neither did they believe that any of these women should be considered for apostleship. They were too late however, because Jesus had already given the women that position. The women should have stood up for what God Himself had ordained, like Paul did.

As a quick aside, what would have happened to Captain Naaman, a man of great authority, if he had disregarded the advise of his little slave girl, a female, the way Peter and the other disciples disregarded the eye witness account of Mary and the women? This man of great authority would have died a pitiful leper. Without even being a "believer," this wise man humbled himself to the wisdom and "authority of faith" of this female child and received his miraculous healing. The story is found in 2 Kings 5.

Interestingly, Apostle Paul, who was not one of the disciples, repeatedly refers to himself as an apostle. And we all accept him as such. But he too was not "voted in" like Matthias was. You may want to read what Paul says of himself, his work and his title as found in Romans 1:1, Galatians 1:1, 10 and 11; 1 Corinthians 1:1 and 2 Corinthians 1:1. And let us remember that Paul is the man who accepts, encourages and celebrates women and the work of women, referring to them as apostles, elders, deacons and fellow laborers. Paul and the women were of kindred spirit.

Therefore, since we know that Mary and other women were disciples of Jesus; and since we know that Jesus Himself chose to appear to the women disciples first, and not to the male disciples; and since we know that Jesus also commissioned these women to carry the "good news" of His resurrection to the others; and since we know that women participated in the organization, planting and growth of the Christian church and were martyrs just like men were, then we should readily understand the truth that Mary and these female disciples were definitely apostles just as the men were. These women were apostles indeed. They were called by God. I wonder whether one of the problems Peter had with Paul was that the Pauline community embraced its active women as apostles, deacons and church leaders.

Getting back to the authorship of the book of Hebrews, perhaps this exclusive list is a function of the attitudinal and cultural limitation of its writer. Maybe the author was careful not to offend the Jews to whom the book of Hebrews was written. Or perhaps this writer did not think it important to render an exhaustive listing.

Or perhaps the author was more impressed with Sarah being the matriarch through whom the Hebrew nation was borne. And as stated earlier, God gave Sarah her new name and her own promise of dominion independent of Abraham's name and promise. Perhaps this is what impressed the writer to single out Sarah.

The writer also included Rahab and referred to her as "harlot." Yet this woman who saved the Israelite soldiers was counted as faithful in God's eyes, and became an ancestor of our Savior. In religious tradition we are reminded of certain women's past sins by tagging them with a title reflecting their "before Christ behavior." These infamous titles and deeds are also kept fresh in our minds by the sermons we hear today. Why is this? Why don't we remove the title of Apostle, from the names Paul and Peter, and the title of Saint from the names Matthew, Mark, Luke and John? So instead of Apostle Paul, we would read or say, "Persecutor Paul" and "Profane Peter." We always hear and talk about "Prostitute Mary" or "Harlot

Rahab." What hypocrisy. I have not found in the Bible any statement implying that Mary was a prostitute anyway. But what would Jesus say? What did He say concerning these women's past? We need to be like Jesus, especially if we profess to be Christians.

But now let us look at another reason why these two wonderful women must have stood out in the writer's mind. You see, they represent the full circle of salvation and the message of the gospel. It is by studying the attitude and life of Sarah that we enter into Christology. By allowing Abraham to lie about her marital status, Sarah showed her willingness to give her life for the one she loved. She was willing to be prostituted to save her frightened husband's life. Back in those days, a king could take any female family member from anyone's home. If the man refused, he could be killed. This was especially true of an alien in that country. So Abraham thought if he told King Abimelech, of Egypt, that Sarah was his sister instead of his wife, the king would spare his life. Sarah consented to this charade because she loved her husband and trusted in the God of the covenant. Sarah's self-sacrificial and loving attitude had a positive influence on Abraham. When God later asked Abraham to sacrifice his son Isaac, he exhibited the same level of trust in God that Sarah had shown earlier. So we see in Sarah the revelation of Christ who offered himself for the safety and salvation of humankind.

Then there is Rahab, a converted "lady of the night," who cooperated with the God of the Israelites and joined the covenant life. Rahab represents sinners who hear the call of God, the truth as it is in Jesus, and obey. They are then grafted into the family of God and receive their covenant rights, their blessings as heirs of God and joint-heirs with Christ (Romans 8:17; Galatians 4:7).

The writer included these two women in the Bible's hall of faith. Perhaps it is because their lives and attitudes revealed and foreshadowed the essence of the gospel. For in the gospel there must be the Savior, represented as Sarah, and there must be the sinner, represented as Rahab. These two women indeed represent the truth of the full gospel message. They complete the circle of love.

Apostle Paul did have more of an open mind and spirit. Perhaps this was why he was chosen by God to write almost two-thirds of the New Testament without being one of Jesus' disciples, and without ever witnessing one of Jesus' miracles. We know that Apostle Paul was an educated, confident, and converted man who wrote the most about women's work in the church. Paul surrounds himself with women who are dedicated, hard working, educated and gifted with leadership skills. Such women Paul commends highly in the New Testament. He refers to Phoebe, a female, as a church deacon, rather than as a "deaconess." Paul introduces her to the church in Rome as *diakonos*, deacon, not deaconess. Modern translations use deaconess in place of this Greek masculine noun. Paul makes no such distinction. Phoebe the deacon, a woman, carries the same title, authority and responsibilities that any other person would carry having the same title. Paul refers to himself as *diakonos* as well as some other men, such as Timothy, Tychicus, Apollos and Epaphras. Jesus Christ is referred to as a *diakonos* in Romans 15:8. The term deacon is used today in reference to a layman who carries out certain non-ministerial duties. But in the early Christian church this term was used in reference to a minister of the gospel and full-time church official, a publicly recognized church leader.

In Romans 16:6 Paul refers to Mary as one who labored much. He uses this same term in reference to his own labor. See 1 Corinthians 15:10, Galatians 4:11 and Philippians 2:16.

Paul commends Junia, a woman, for being a great *apostle* in Romans 16:7. So as Paul has shown us, by his example of leadership, the office of apostle was not at all gender dependent. Paul established the Christian church on the truth that both men and women alike have the same origin, the same destiny, the same sinfulness and the same hope. The also have the same commission to spread the gospel message. The book, *Why Not Women*, by Christian scholars, Loren Cunningham and David Joel Hamilton gives an excellent review on early Church history relating to Paul and women leaders.

It is very interesting to read Romans 10:6-9 in which Paul speaks on the work of the Holy Spirit as he tells the Christian church in Rome of his hopes for the Jews embracing the gospel. Please take time to read these texts now, and follow along in your Bible to get the maximum benefit. It appears that he is taking a stand to defend his ministry method that heavily involves women as preachers and church leaders. This would have been forbidden in the Jewish synagogues. The NIV reads like this, "But the righteousness that is by faith says: Do not say in your heart, Who will ascend into heaven? (that is, to bring Christ down) or Who will descend into the deep? (that is, to bring Christ up from the dead). But what does it say? The word is near you; it is in your mouth and in your heart, that is, the word of faith we are proclaiming: That if you confess with your mouth, Jesus is Lord, and believe in your heart that God raised him from the dead, you will be saved." Paul addresses the work of the

Holy Spirit as it relates to gospel message. The Holy Spirit is female. The Jews would have had a big problem with this truth.

King David, the most noted king of Israel, refers to women as those who proclaim the gospel, preachers. And Paul, the most noted Christian church leader and New Testament author, also refers to women as preachers. What wonderful similarity. And of course, if you read Isaiah 52: 7 and 10 you will see very similar passages concerning those carrying the good tidings as well as the revelation of the Holy Spirit. Here we find that the King James Version of the Bible replaces the pronoun "those" found in the original Hebrew, with the word "him" in verse 7. Again, a pronoun that could include females (and does indeed refer to females) is changed to a masculine pronoun. We have learned that it is the Holy Spirit who brought Jesus from heaven to earth. It is the Holy Spirit who raised Jesus from the dead. Paul is trying to show them the person of the Holy Spirit. In the following verses, 14-16, Paul talks about the mission of preachers while also referring to Scripture found in Psalms 68:11b, where women are the ones proclaiming good tidings, according to the original Hebrew translation. He also refers to Isaiah 53:1 in which the Holy Spirit is called *she*. Psalms 68:11 and 12 continue to talk of women's activities and use the illustration of the female dove. The dove is symbolic of the Holy Spirit, the female God in the Trinity. So Paul is actually referring to women as preachers of the gospel, just as was written in the Psalms. He is also referring to the Holy Spirit as being involved in feminine activities. He was hoping that the Jews would "get the picture" of female inclusion, and that these truths would not cause them to reject the gospel message.

In verse 10 the Hebrew translation says that the *arm of Yahweh*, the Holy Spirit, will be laid bare, meaning, to be made known, uncovered or discovered. Her true identity will be unveiled as the good tidings of the gospel and of the Ones who sent Jesus here are carried by "those" women and men "unto all nations" (Matthew 28:19). Please take time to read and study these texts for yourself. We have come to this prophetic season right now as we digest and spread the truths in this book, as it refers to Holy Writ.

The earliest Christian churches had women apostles, deacons, teachers, ministers, founders, and leaders. And why shouldn't they have? In Ephesians 4:11-6 we read of the five-fold ministry of which believers are to participate, according to the gifts given them by the Holy Spirit. She did not only give these gifts to men. She also gives these gifts to women. And there are more women in the Christian church than there are men, even today! So is it at all reasonable to think that only men are to be ministers and church leaders? That doesn't even make sense, any way you look at it. It has been the sinful tradition of men that has hindered women from using their God given gifts in ministry. During the centuries following the establishment of the church, changes were made to exclude women from such service, responsibility, leadership, influence and honor. Satan has always tried to obscure God's foundation of truth and operation. For every truth, there is a counterfeit; for every right, a wrong.

During the time of Christian persecution the Bible was taken from the common people and given to the political Church system, the Church of Rome, for "safe keeping." It was during this time that people were appointed to church leadership and given the sole right to read and to interpret the Bible for the laity. There was simony, the practice of buying and selling church office for money. There was also nepotism, showing favoritism to relatives in appointing them to church office. There were those who secured positions of church leadership even though they were incompetent, power-hungry, ungodly and void of Holy Spirit conviction. Major changes of the original intent of God's Word were made. Furthermore, the Christian church was impacted by cultural influences of its day as Greek and Roman teachings were brought into it. Paul spent a lot of time and energy trying to put out the fire of these schisms.

Remember that the status of women, during that time, was about the same as that of animals and other property. They had no rights and no voice in society. So as these influences crept into the Church, the leadership and authority women exercised earlier were diminished and taken away. The church as a place of refuge from sinful tradition became the place of oppression, condemnation, spiritual and emotional bondage. Let us look at some of these changes:

- Church leadership roles carried out by both men and women were changed to a "men only" rule.
- Ministries of music in churches carried out by both men and women were changed to "men only" formats. According to the author of *The Silent Shout*, Dr. Errol Stoddart's research concerning the evolution of Christian music reveals that women were restricted from participating in the music ministries of church choirs in 578 A.D.
- Other changes include the allowance of the worshipping of images and the veneration of angels, saints, relics, pictures and statues. And according to the book *Christianity Through the Centuries* by Earle E. Cairns, we find that other changes include worship services became more elaborate and showy; a sharp distinction was made between the clergy and laity; Sunday became the favored day of worship.

It seems that the Christian church has never fully recovered from the changes imposed by invading cultural influences and by the rulings of the political Church system around the time of the Middle Ages. There is much information on Christian church history available to those who would like an in-depth look. Protestants and Protestant historians consider this time of change in the Church as a dark age where the early Church was corrupted.

But we know that Jesus, in the Messianic community had women disciples. Women were among the seventy disciples that He sent out to evangelize (see Luke 8:1-3; 10:1, Mark 15:40, 41 then Luke 24:10). Jesus and Paul were alike in that they respected women as well as men. Both of them saw the wisdom and practicality of involving males and females in the work of building up the kingdom of God as this kingdom is made up of both sexes. Both showed that, as believers of the faith, maleness and femaleness are not opposing issues, and that together they reflect the body of Christ—"For in him dwelleth the fulness of the Godhead bodily. And ye are complete in him" (Colossians 2:9, 10).

Jesus and Paul both embraced and encouraged the leadership skills and the ministries of women. Both of them, unhindered by prejudice and bigotry, maximized their potential in ministry.

Jesus and Paul both embraced and encouraged the leadership skills and the ministries of women. Both of them, unhindered by prejudice and bigotry, maximized their potential in ministry. Paul's ministry, establishing the early Christian church, embraced women, such as Priscilla and Nympha, as church leaders. Priscilla taught Apollos, the male evangelist who worked with Paul. Some of the many women who served as church officials and leaders include Tryphaina, Tryphosa, Persis, Nereus's sister, Euodia, Apphia, and Syntyche. Lydia, the first European convert to Christianity, was the leader of the church in Thyatira. She was a professional woman who financially provided for Paul and Silas in ministry (Acts 16: 14,15).

So Apostle Paul and the early Christian church had no problem working with women of the gospel. And of his thirty-nine fellow workers that he mentions by name more than a fourth of them are women! Both Paul and Jesus, extremely bright young men and Spirit-filled, understood that women are necessary participants in the global spread of the gospel. All members of the Christian church have spiritual gifts from the Holy Spirit. So what would it profit the corporate Church to keep women in silence and obscurity when such women are equipped and willing to spread the gospel message? This kind of practice is of satanic origin. It is a hindering spirit. Satan has hindered the spreading of the gospel by influencing men to hinder the ministry of women. This is indeed spiritual warfare.

Apostle Paul persevered in radical ministry against the backdrop of steep religious tradition that demanded female-inferiority ideation. Paul had an anointing of confrontation, which was necessary in his time. If Paul had not confronted religious tradition of his day, the gospel message could not have spread as well as it did. The gospel spread very fast with the help of women's efforts that Paul embraced. And again in this end time, the same confrontation anointing must manifest so that spirituality will replace religious tradition. There are not enough male leaders to finish the work of spreading the gospel. And all leaders are not interested in spreading the gospel. Religious tradition is the greatest hindrance to revival. It is the mode of operation used by religious leaders to retain their position on the prominent and prideful patriarchal pedestal.

It is time for such leaders to understand their servant status in the church. The time has come for them to remember the fact that the church is the bride of Christ, because it belongs to Christ and not to them. It is time for them to put down their burden of politics and pettiness and personal agenda, and pick up the burden of the Lord for precious souls to be converted by Holy Ghost revival. Christ's yoke is easy and His burden is light, because they are not heavy laden with the weight of male egotism and self promotion.

Business as usual is not good enough. Business as usual will not get the job done. Women and men alike must become righteously indignant with the stagnant status quo system in the church.

Women are natural communicators and influencers. If there are any to be released into ministry, it should be women. Jesus, Paul and David knew this truth and used it to their advantage in spreading good tidings to all people. Paul speaks of the spiritual battle involved in Christian growth, activity and ministry. Ephesians 6:12 says, "For we wrestle not against flesh and blood, but against principalities, against powers, against the rulers of the darkness of this world, against spiritual wickedness in high places." Satan realized long ago that finding a way to silence good communicators and influencers in gospel work would give his kingdom of darkness a great advantage. He found such a way by having the ministries of women silenced by men who profess Christianity.

God said in Micah 6:4 and Exodus 15:20-21 that three great leaders for the Hebrew nation were Moses, Aaron, and Miriam. He chose not to exclude Miriam. Why would He? God celebrates what should be celebrated. He celebrates His own creation. He is fair.

Women have been leaders throughout the Old and New Testament times. The name Mary comes from the name Miriam. And it is very interesting that Miriam protected the deliverer, Moses, her baby brother, in the land of Egypt after his birth; and Mary protected the Deliverer, Jesus Christ, her baby, in the land of Egypt after his birth. There were several of Jesus' followers with the name Mary, including his own mother. God was indeed making a statement by choosing a Mary to mother His only begotten Son, and another Mary to tell the others of the resurrection of His only begotten Son. These names serve as symbols of life-giving, of nurturing, of dominion and of freedom.

Jesus came and affirmed God's view of the woman during a time when women were only tolerated and not celebrated in the Jewish, Roman and Greek cultures. After Jesus ascended to heaven, and only after the Holy Spirit fell on His disciples in the upper room, did Peter pay attention to Jesus' stance concerning gender relations in the gospel proclamation. Then and only then does Peter refer to Joel's prophecy concerning the Spirit being poured out on all flesh, an all-gender ministry and an all-inclusive Christian community. You may review Acts 1:12- 2:18. Peter should have put action behind his proclamation.

Chapter Ten

Family Names

Let's Study Manasseh

Now let me tell you about another dream I had during the season of fasting and prayer in 2002. One night I dreamed that I had an appointment to speak at a church. When my family and I arrived we were ushered to the front row. While walking I began to look for my notes, but could not find them. I asked Maurice to look in his belongings, but he did not have the notes either. While searching further, I sent my daughter to the pulpit to give a speech; and she did very well. Then I was introduced and took my place.

First, I led the congregation in singing a beautiful song. Then the audience began to clap and praise God and worship. It was a wonderful experience. During that time of praise and glorifying God, the title of my topic came to mind. The topic was about Manasseh, but I still didn't have any notes. I prayed in my heart for God to reveal to me the what, who or the where of Manasseh. Then a voice said, "Go and study Manasseh." I immediately awakened in a sweat, and my heart was racing. I got up and ran to the family library where I began to discover "Manasseh."

The first thing I studied was the life of Joseph, Son of Jacob and Rachael. At an early age, Joseph endured a life of hurt and rejection by his own people, his brothers. After going through his process of purification successfully, God more than restored him. He brought Joseph into the complete manifestation of the dreams that He had deposited into his spirit. But at each stage of the process Joseph maintained the right attitude. He held on to his faith in God even though his path seemed dark. Joseph learned to "walk by faith and not by sight" (2 Corinthians 5:7). He held to his principles as a young man of integrity and to his faith in God.

When Joseph was restored and began to live in abundance, he and his wife, Princess Asenath, had their first son. Joseph named him Manasseh. The name means "to forget" or "to forgive." He named the second son Ephraim. This name means "fruitful" or "doubly fruitful." So what Joseph was modeling concerning the history of his life and to benefit us today is that before fruitfulness comes to us, we must forgive the ills of our past. That is also what Jesus Christ modeled and prayed about while here on this earth. He taught us to pray, "Forgive us our debts as we forgive our debtors" (Matthew 6:12).

Not forgiving will delay and even abort our fruitfulness. We cannot reach our greatest potential in this life without applying the law of forgiveness. So God was telling me to let go of all the past hurts I was holding on to and to forgive those who had injured me. Only then could He take me to a much greater level of success and fruitfulness. Only then could God move me from success to significance, from productivity to power—power that comes from the Holy Spirit.

The Manasseh story and name are what women absolutely must know, understand and apply in order to get to the place of their rightful dominion as a daughter of Deity and as a queen on the earth. Apostle Paul puts it this way: "Forgetting those things which are behind, and reaching forth unto those things which are before, I press toward the mark for the prize of the high calling of God in Christ Jesus" (Philippians 3:13, 14).

The second lesson I learned from the study of Manasseh is found in Numbers 27:1-7. Let us read this awesome story:

"Then came the daughters of Zelophehad, the son of Manasseh of the families of Manasseh the son of Joseph; and these are the names of his daughters: Mahlah, Noah, Hoglah, Milcah and Tirzah. And they stood before Moses, and before Eleazar the priest, and before the princes, and all of the congregation, by the door of the tabernacle of the congregation saying, 'Our father died in the wilderness, and he was not in the company of them that gathered themselves together against the Lord in the company of Korah; but died in his own sin, and had no sons. Why should the name of our father be done away from among his family, because he hath no son? Give unto us therefore a possession among the brethren of our father.' And Moses brought their cause before the Lord, And the Lord spake unto Moses, saying, 'The *daughters* of Zelophehad speak right: thou shalt surely give them a possession of an inheritance among their father's brethren; and thou shalt cause the inheritance of their father to pass unto them.'"

Traditions of man had determined that the woman had no inheritance, no dominion except that which came from her husband, if married, or some other male authority figure. Then God provided a way for this custom to be challenged into a more inclusive practice. Zelophehad was the great, great, great grandson of Manasseh, Joseph's son. He had no sons. He had five daughters. Each of the names he gave them had a meaning, according to the *Bible Dictionary and Concordance* (Broadman and Holman Publishers: Nashville, TN 1998).

Mahlah means "disease and sickness."

Noah means "tremble, quiver, waver."

Hoglah means "the end of mourning and sadness, family, descendents, household, to take refuge." Reference: John 16:20, 21.

Milcah means "queen or counsel."

Tirzah means "charm and delight."

It seems that Zelophehad named his daughters prophetically. I see these names as stages through which the female gender will journey to get to the place of Divine intention:

Mahlah: Implies that something is wrong with the female gender. This notion, spun by Lucifer, was offered and accepted into the mind of Adam right after sin entered the family. Lucifer told Adam that the woman was his problem. Adam, as he stood in shame behind the tree, blurted this satanic idea to God.

Noah: Because the *mahlah* lie was propagated through family lines, the woman was devalued and was viewed as having limited purpose, like a "quivering wanderer," name of the second daughter, Noah. And this lie has spread worldwide throughout the ages and is, in many ways, quite prevalent today.

Hoglah. With the birth of his third daughter, Zelophehad is beginning to open his spirit to the Spirit of God, the third person of the Godhead. Zelophehad begins to see the light of truth and to gain hope for his own future, propagating his own name through his daughters. He begins to understand the godly value of the female.

He now understands that in the godly family and household the woman can find a place of refuge and rest from the mistreatment of the sinful world. And it is through the "seed of the woman," Jesus, that the her rightful place on this earth will be restored.

We are in the *hoglah* era. As we receive more and more revelation from the Word of God through Holy Spirit Mother, both women and men are beginning to understand the true value of the woman as a "shadow of the heavenly" Woman. I am submitting this book borne of a dream that was deposited into my spirit by my Mother, Holy Spirit Mother, during a 43-day fast into which I was called. The seed of truth was deposited into my spirit after my own daughter, my descendent, in our home, my place of refuge, questioned me about the truth of God as Mother.

As we receive more and more revelation from the Word of God through Holy Spirit Mother, both women and men are beginning to understand the true value of the woman as a "shadow of the heavenly" Woman.

Milcah: The Holy Spirit is beginning to speak louder and show Her identity even more than in times past, as we prepare for the second coming of Jesus Christ. We are entering into the "latter rain" season. And as we grasp this truth of God, we will see ourselves as the royalty God made us. For we are children of the Most High God. The Spirit will be poured out in the last days, on *all* flesh—male and female, young and old. We all will unite to finish the work of spreading the gospel to usher in the new age, the eternal Kingdom of Light. Jesus has "called us out of darkness into His marvelous light" (2Peter 2:9). He is the triune connection to our original Edenic state, before sin.

Tirzah: We are "a holy nation, a royal priesthood." Only as we really learn it, think it, speak it and live it, teach it and sing it, will we then come to the final stage, meaning "charm, delight." As believers in Elohim, the Trinity, accept the truth that the Holy Spirit is indeed the feminine God, then the earthly female and the spirit of woman will also be accepted, embraced and celebrated as she was created to be.

Just as these five unified, brave, persevering sisters stood together with one voice to speak up for what was rightfully theirs and received it with God's blessing, so we must in unity of purpose, with perseverance, and with one voice speak out against gender discrimination in our families, schools, churches, workplace—every area of existence all around the globe. Women must get what is rightfully theirs, beginning with the realization that they have representation in the Godhead. And the blessings of God will surely rest upon them. Our families can then be restored.

Victory is summed up with these two verses, 1 Peter 5:10, 12: "But the God of all grace, who hath called us unto his eternal glory by Christ Jesus, after that ye have suffered a while, make you perfect, establish, strengthen, settle you. To Him be glory and dominion forever and ever. Amen." These are five things God wants to do for women, just as He did for the five daughters of Zelophehad:

He is perfecting and maturing women.

God is calling women.

He is establishing women.

He is strengthening women.

And He is aiming to settle them in their rightful place here on earth as He ordained at creation.

But what if the five sisters had not spoken up? What if they could not come to an agreement of their rightful inheritance? What if some of them spoke up and some refused or even spoke against it? What if some of them were comfortable with the sinful tradition of female exclusion and defended this kind of culture, as some women do today? What impact would they have had on the princes, priest, congregation, and Moses? Or what if they had just allowed things to go on as they always had, during and before their lifetime and thrown their hands up in hopelessness? What if they had accepted the reassignment by men and the devaluation placed on them by men?

They Heard and Obeyed

Unassertive sisters refusing to follow Holy Spirit Mother's promptings would have forfeited their future, their standing in the community, their heritage and their image of Manasseh's tribal identity. They would have relinquished their rightful dominion.

And you can be sure that their demands and petitions were not welcomed and embraced by everyone present. I can just imagine what these young ladies had to suffer through before hearing the final decision. Because thousands of years later, women still are suffering through the process and the pain of trying to effect positive change for themselves. Even Moses, the chosen man of God, the national leader, did not know what to do. But he did have the nobility of character to perceive that there was something more at stake than a plot of property. His open-mindedness and insight made him a good choice for leadership. God is all wise! God had chosen a man He could count on. An average man would have ruled by sight—the natural way of looking at an issue. But Moses ruled by insight—the supernatural way of looking at an issue. So instead of making a hasty decision, and instead of scratching out a sermon motivated by male ego and "works of the flesh" to denounce their petition, he took their case to the Lord. Moses wanted to do what was right and just and fair. He was not at all concerned with being in the "ole boys club." He was a man of integrity.

Only after Moses called on God for guidance did God immediately reply that the women were speaking truth. God said to Moses, "The daughters…speak right." He told Moses to give them their land and property inheritance. If any of these women were married, her own husband would have still been responsible for providing for her as well. If they were not married, they would not lose what they had inherited by getting married. Which means that marriage does not demand women to give up their own dominion. This is not to say that everything will remain exactly the same. When two adults unite, both parties must make some adjustments. But if the wife is the only one making adjustments and compromises, I can tell you now that she has not done herself any favors. So these five wise women did what was right for themselves and received their own blessing, and their own inheritance. This is quite similar to the blessed life of the virtuous woman in Proverbs 31. These women knew how to live well. And God was pleased!

Only after Moses called on God for guidance did God immediately reply that the women were speaking truth. God said to Moses, "The daughters…speak right."

Human beings are God's mouthpiece on this earth. If we don't speak it and call it out, God will keep silent in most instances. He does not want us to be complacent, lazy, and idle. He does not want us to take life as it is handed to us. He wants us to take a stand for the right, which is a stand against the wrong. God would not have brought the Israelites out of Egyptian bondage without the effort and cooperation of human beings. God would not have brought the American system of slavery and other oppressive regimes around the world to an end without the effort of human beings.

So the five daughters of Zelophehad changed their circumstance to one of victory that still benefits men and women today. Laws were changed because of their courage; and modern civilizations have used these same laws in their own system. And just as in the case of these women, God will not effect positive change for women around the world without their effort. It is the duty of all adults, women and men, to gather knowledge and to exercise courage to build and effect positive change. The Bible says, "My people are destroyed for lack of knowledge" (Hosea 4:6). "Wisdom is the principal thing.... And with all thy getting, get understanding" (Proverbs 4:7). *Get* denotes action on our part requiring effort and sacrifice. To lack knowledge is to be in darkness. The Word of God illuminates the spirit and the mind about His thoughts and will for His children.

You don't have to walk in darkness:

Psalms 119:105. "Thy word is a lamp unto my feet and a light unto my path."

Proverbs 4:18. "But the path of the just is as a shining light, that shineth more and more unto the perfect day."

Isaiah 5:20-24 "Woe unto them that call evil good, and good evil; that put darkness for light, and light for darkness; that put bitter for sweet, and sweet for bitter! Woe unto them that are wise in their own eyes, and prudent in their own sight! Which justify the wicked for reward, and take away the righteousness of the righteous from him! Therefore as the fire devoureth the stubble, and the flame consumeth the chaff, so their root shall be as rottenness, and their blossom shall go up as dust: because they have cast away the law of the Lord of hosts, and despised the word of the Holy One of Israel." The family unit has been falling apart by root-rot because its foundation of identity with God has been spoiled. When God's image is restored at the foundation, for each of its members, the family unit will be restored to godliness.

1 John 1:7. "But if we walk in the light, as He is in the light, we have fellowship one with another, and the blood of Jesus Christ His Son cleanseth us from all sin." Fellowship is what the Christian family must experience, not lord-and-subject type of relationship.

Ephesians 5:6-11, 17. "Let no man deceive you with vain words: for because of these things cometh the wrath of God upon the children of disobedience. Be not ye therefore partakers with them. For ye were sometimes darkness, but now are ye light in the Lord: walk as children of light: (for the fruit of the Spirit is in all goodness and righteousness and truth;) proving what is acceptable unto the Lord. And have no fellowship with the unfruitful works of darkness, but rather reprove them. Wherefore be ye not unwise, but understanding what the will of the Lord is." We must come to the place of dissatisfaction with the way things are presently in gender relations, act for positive change and never look back. The time is now, the place is here and the person is you. What are you going to do with the light you now have?

John 8:12. Jesus says, "I am the light of the world: he that followeth me shall not walk in darkness, but shall have the light of life."

In these times, as in any time in history, any woman, married or not, has a God-given right to have her own dominion, her own identity, her own education, and her own career (when feasible in light of raising young children). I am quite aware that there are some women who choose not to go this route. There are some women whose life's goal is to marry. Once they have achieved this goal, nothing else matters. My appeal is not to them. I am happy for those who are happy with that kind of life. However, according to God's Word and according to the name God gave the woman in Eden, motherhood as depicted by the name Eve, is not enough; just as fatherhood is not enough for Adam-male. And I would also admonish these women to be happy for the women who want more in life. There are women who desire to "have it all," all that God ordained at creation. That is, they desire to have and nurture family, earn an education, have a career, and be successful and significant in service and in their own dominion. This is God's command, according to Genesis 1:27, 28 and Genesis 5:2.

We discussed the five daughter of Zelophehad. Now let us talk about another family of women. Did you know that after Job's trial and restoration, he begat three daughters? They were named *Jemima*, which means, "daylight or restored", *Keren-Happuch,* which signifies beauty, and *Kezia,* which means "fragrance of a flower" or penetrating influence. These names that Job gave his daughters tell me how he felt about women and the insight he had about the spirit of woman. The spirit of woman is that of creativity and restoration, beauty and influence. We have already visited Scripture relating to the characteristics and ministry of the Holy Spirit and how She is the model for Her daughters, women made in Her image and likeness. And Job gave his daughters an inheritance of property and land just as he did for his sons. No wonder God trusted him and bragged on him. He knew this man was untraditional, fair, progressive, and godly— untainted by the culture and tradition of his time.

A woman should not be known solely for her husband's accomplishments—they belong to him. She should make a name for herself and a heritage for her children. And certainly when it comes to recognition and respect for those women who have chosen to accomplish their own works as individuals, she should receive sole credit. If this poses a problem for some people, it is simply because they harbor jealousy and malice toward women. Usually such people—men and women— are not accomplished, therefore are intimidated and perhaps jealous too. Then there are others, who may indeed be accomplished, and feel that women should not be. But in any case, as we have studied, this is not God's way.

I can only speak of myself in this regard, drawing from a few of many, many personal experiences with those who have exhibited such fear. Having been blessed to become a licensed, practicing physician before marrying, I also became a board certified Emergency Medicine physician shortly afterward. And while concentrating on my work, not looking for a husband, Maurice found me.

Having been an active member of the church since childhood, I continue to be an active member in the church community. There have been some leaders, in churches where I have served, who refuse to use the proper and earned title of women in a public setting. If this were their general way of doing things for both male and female, then I would understand. However, such is not the case. They have miserably failed on such a simple and basic matter. But this is merely a symptom of a deeper lying sickness. These leaders never hesitate to give proper title and due respect to the male professionals in the same setting. So in an effort to understand this kind of thought process, this kind of tradition, I confronted one such pastor. I am only writing about this particular one of the several pastors to whom I have spoken concerning this issue. His obvious practice of withholding due respect from females was affecting the attitude of other local church leaders and laymen alike, especially the young men.

After speaking with him on this issue, a higher-ranking church leader, from another state, telephoned me the following day. He counseled me against trying to make such a simple yet positive change for women. He promised me that things would "get much worse" for me before they would get better if I pursued positive change. He also stated that this issue would never be improved for women in this particular church organization. He said that I should just accept it. Did he sound like the godly Moses? I respectfully let him know that his counsel was heard and rejected. Interestingly enough, this church official is the person who molested me as a teenager; and I did report it. His view of the female is understandable in light of his behavior against females. Therefore he would feel quite comfortable giving me this "warning." Let me add here, I have forgiven him and continue in my God-given assignments.

God says not to have fellowship with darkness. Darkness is anything or anyone willingly operating outside of the truth of God. Obviously this includes religious tradition too. I told this minister that "no weapon formed" against me would prosper (Isaiah 54:17). And that He who has begun a good work in me is faithful to complete it (Philippians 1:6)! I am available to God to affect positive change. Sacrifice is the price of change. Change is the reward for sacrifice! But woe unto him by which persecution comes. Yes, I am willing to pay the price for my daughter's and my own inheritance, as well as for women everywhere and future generations. I rejoice to be counted worthy to suffer for the kingdom of God. And I know that God is taking note of those who persecute others, according to 2 Thessalonians 1:4b-12. Please take a look at these texts. Additionally we find in Romans 8:18 that the reward outweighs the trouble: "For I reckon that the sufferings of this present time are not worthy to be compared with the glory which shall be revealed in us." The pain is not in vain. "Weeping may endure for a night, but joy cometh in the morning" (Psalms 30:5).

Unlike the godly leader, Moses, such people don't seem to understand that this simple issue runs much deeper than a title. This kind of bias and disrespect is really against the Creator, because women are made in God's image. And it is by God's provision and direction that women have chosen and have accomplished certain goals in life, which benefit the church and the world. Therefore, such people are really discrediting and trying to silence the blessings of God to women, while they celebrate His blessings to men. These are the people who seek to undermine and discount the authority, influence and rightful dominion of the woman. This attitude is manifested in many different ways—not just the title issue. Do they ever stop to inquire what the will of the Lord is on this issue, as Moses did? Are they so hardened and set in their own ways that only divine intervention will force their hand? I do pity them if such is the case, because when God steps in, it will be worse than if they would humble themselves before the mighty hand of the Lord (1 Peter 5:6). And I wonder whether or not these same people would refuse medical care from a female physician if they were having a heart attack, a stroke, or an anaphylactic reaction? Taking a stand for the right is the right stand to take. Women must stand and walk and live in their full authority as daughters of the Most High God.

Isaiah 63:7. "I will mention the loving kindness of the Lord, and the praises of the Lord, according to all that the Lord hath bestowed on us (male and female), and the great goodness toward the house of Israel [the church]."

James 3:10, 17. Concerning the tongue, attitude, and wisdom in the church: "Out of the same mouth proceedeth blessing and cursing. My brethren, these things ought not so to be" (v. 10). "But the wisdom that is from above is first pure, then peaceable, gentle, and easy to be intreated, full of mercy and good fruits, without partiality, and without hypocrisy" (v. 17).

Isaiah 2:17. "The loftiness (haughtiness and pride) of man shall be made low, and the Lord alone shall be exalted in that day."

According to the book *What Does the Bible Say About...*, of Thomas Nelson's A to Z series, Jewish tradition in Jesus' day was against the woman being formally educated, and it was especially against them being enrolled in the schools of the rabbis. Women were allowed to sit in the outer area or the back of the synagogues, away from the men. Women were considered the cause of sexual sins that men engaged in. Again, here we see the generational iniquity of men passed on from Adam-man, the first blamer. Therefore men were not allowed to speak to, nor have any physical contact with a woman in public.

But in direct contrast to these traditions, Jesus taught both men and women. Jesus spoke to women in public as seen in John 4:27 and in other places documented in the Bible. Jesus touched women in public (Mark 5:41). And when Jesus met the woman who was about to be stoned to death for adultery, He defended her, forgave her, empowered her to change, did not condemn her and exposed her accusers' worse sins.

Jesus came to show us a new and better way of living and thinking. And in contrast to the Old Testament Ceremonial Law, Jesus gave us a new covenant and showed that through Him, we all have equal access to God and equal rights as God-appointed heirs of this earth.

Jesus had a circle of followers, supporters and disciples according to Luke 23:48,49 while here on this earth. He educated His female followers just as He did His male followers (Luke 23: 49). In reading of the Holy Word we see that He used illustrations and parables that both sexes could identify with. He also used illustrations that assigned male as well as female activities and imagery with Deity.

So the point here is that there's nothing wrong with anyone, male or female getting an education. It is nothing to be ashamed of, nothing to be persecuted and put down about, and nothing to try to hide and keep in a corner. Anything that is a put down, is not of God, no matter who does the putting down and no matter what disguise is used with it- a sermon, joke, or tradition.

Anything that is a put down, is not of God, no matter who does the putting down and no matter what disguise is used with it- a sermon, joke, or tradition.

Women have equal access to Jesus, the Source of power that is infinite, immaculate, and irrefutable. And Holy Spirit Mother is always on the side of right, whether male or female. And "if God be for us, who can be against us?" (Romans 8:31).

The Bible assures that "When the enemy (spirit of division, inequity, polarity, bigotry, superiority ideation which all originate from the enemy of souls) shall come in like a flood, the Spirit of the Lord (Mother) shall lift up a standard against him" (Isaiah 59:19).

We are protected. We are defended. We are shielded. "Not by might, nor by power; but by my spirit, saith the Lord of hosts" (Zechariah 4:6).

So, "The joy of the Lord is your strength" (Nehemiah 8:10). Jesus came to show the world God's assigned value on the woman, and it perfectly contradicts the value with which man has tried to reassign her. Women must choose the better value. Jesus came to set women free—free to be themselves, free to be who He made them to be (John 8:6).

There is power in vision, in unity, in perseverance, and in the tongue. But most of all there is wonder working power in the blood of Jesus, the spotless Lamb of God. And "with God all things are possible" (Mark 10:27). Glory Hallelujah. A new day is birthed! "This is the day that the Lord has made; we will rejoice and be glad in it" (Psalms 118:24). "Let the redeemed of the Lord say so" (Psalms 107:2).

Because of the dreams I had concerning Jesus' attitude toward women and of the true identity of the Holy Spirit without ever having heard of this information during my lifetime, I thought that I was venturing into the "unknown alone." And even though discovering Scriptures that reveal the truth of the Holy Spirit along with other supportive documents, I still desired a partnership of sort in reference to the Holy Spirit in terms of feminine deity. As I was about to submit this manuscript for publication, through another divine appointment, the work of the renowned 18th century aristocrat and German theologian, Count Zinzendorf was introduced to me. So I readily decided to insert his information right here. Having never heard of this wonderful man in any of the Bible courses I have taken in school, I trembled with excitement and gratitude while reading about his life and the revelation he too received from God concerning the identity of the Holy Spirit in the year 1738. He referred to the Holy Spirit as "mother."

Count Zinzendorf, leader of the Moravian religious organization, was responsible for the first Protestant missionary work, allowing the gospel of Jesus to be spread to the West Indies, America, Africa, Russia and other parts of the world. He was also influential in the life and work of the reformists, Jan Hus and John Wesley, whom we have all heard about. I believe that even though never attending a theological seminary, Zinzendorf made some of the greatest impacts on the world because of his dedication to God, his love for Jesus and his openness to the Holy Spirit. He embraced the Godhead as a family unit. He wrote that he did not talk much about his belief of the Holy Spirit being "mother" because he did not know how to really explain this concept, and that he only had an abstract understanding of this truth. In his church community, there were women ministers, bishops and deacons. This man reminds me of Apostle Paul, King David and Jesus.

Holy Spirit Mother God is marvelous, magnificent and majestic. She is more worthy than our highest praise could ever render. And, yes, we are our Mother's children. So now that we know just who the Holy Spirit really is, we can better understand the role and responsibility of godly women who follow the model of their heavenly Mother. With this in mind, let me share a speech that I wrote for my daughter to share with multitudes everywhere. The truth is that where feminine representation in the Godhead is understood and embraced, the spirit of woman is also understood, embraced and celebrated. When this representation is believed and understood every individual family can become unified and strong, because the true value of each family member is present. Therefore, gender problems would no longer exist to hinder us from our full expression in godliness within the family. And we would experience God's peace in reflecting heaven on earth. "Thy will be done on earth as it is in heaven." And now, the speech:

Spirit Of Woman

If this generation of women today would only protect, preserve, and propagate the true spirit of woman, my generation will indeed have what it needs to press on in prosperity, in profit and in peace.

Woman in its original meaning, its earliest position, means "Mother of all living, female of productivity, blessing and dominion." *Woman* denotes beginnings, creativity, originality, propagation, sustenance, and strength. So there is no wonder that the pronoun *she* is used to refer to things that are held in high regard, things that are beneficial, things that are great, things that are valuable, and things that are worthy. The large, stately, seaworthy vessel that is used for the safe passage of life across the oceans is referred to as "she." Any grand machine is used to make needed goods or to perform essential services. It creates commodities of comfort. It supports profit and prosperity. It is referred to as "she." The United States of America is referred to as "she" to reflect the spirit of the tenacious women that bore, cared for, and nurtured its people.

So you can see that the very essence of woman, her spirit, is everywhere and in all. Her essence is essential to life and all living things:

The spirit of woman is expected and is eternal.

The spirit of woman affects all and influences all.

The spirit of woman creates so that others may exist.

The spirit of woman guides all and develops all.

The spirit of woman initiates so that others may imitate.

The spirit of woman nurtures all and protects all.

The spirit of woman picks up where others leave off.

The spirit of woman surrounds all and penetrates all.

The spirit of woman births greatness.

The spirit of woman is the most powerful influence on earth, next to God. It is the very spirit of woman that has molded and helped to shape cultures of every age. In fact, it is the hand of or the spirit of woman, which rocks the cradle and shapes the world.

So where there is a need for beginnings, a need for change, a need for progress, a need for influence, a need for steadfast leadership, and, yes, where there is a need for the promise of greatness, just look to the spirit of woman! For the essence of life and living is embodied by her spirit. And that spirit lives forever! Thank you. Amen.

It's Harvest Time

What a difference females could make in their communities and all around the world, if they would tap into the power that flows from standing with others of like vision, in unity, and in perseverance. By using the power of the tongue and taking a stand to make a difference, women will indeed get all that belong to them.

The Holy Bible tells us what is rightfully ours having been created in the image and likeness of God. But what we hear and receive into our spirit, determines our harvest. So if women hear the Word but put limits on the Word for their life because of preconceived ideas, then their harvest will be meager. They will absolutely not receive the abundant life God has provided through Jesus Christ. This truth is brought out in the parable of the seed and the sower of Mark 4:3-24. Take time to read this and research its meaning. Then concentrate on the last few verses, 20-24: "'And these are they which are sown on good ground; such as hear the word, and receive it, and bring forth fruit, some thirty-fold, some sixty and some an hundred.' And he said unto them, 'Is a candle brought to be put under a bushel, or under a bed? And not to be set on a candlestick? For there is nothing hid, which shall not be manifested; neither was any thing kept secret, but that it should come abroad. If any man have ears to hear, let him hear.' And he said unto them, 'Take heed what ye hear: with what measure ye mete, it shall be measured to you; and unto you that hear shall more be given.'"

What Jesus is telling us in this parable is that, if we receive God's thoughts and words into our life, without limiting that word for ourselves and other people, we will be given more and more revelation knowledge and power that comes through that knowledge. If we put limits on God's word in our life, we will not receive a decent harvest at all. We will be in lack of what He has to offer as found in His living Word. "My people are destroyed for lack of knowledge." Don't let this be you.

The Holy Spirit's Work

Sweet Holy Spirit, please minister to us:
Lead us, guide us, instruct us, and show us.
Tell us, convict us, fix us, and grow us.
Counsel us, improve us, make us, and mold us.
Enlighten us, refine us, polish us, and control us.
Fill us, empower us, energize us, and interpose for us.
Then confidently use us in Your work.

So work on us.
Work in us.
Work with us.
And work for us.
Then work thru us,
So that we can help others
Who are where we were
Before You came to us.
Thank you for believing in us.
In the name of Jesus, Amen!

Chapter Eleven

Family Walk

You have read the truth that every created human being has God-given dominion on this earth, both man and woman. You have seen from the Bible that the woman was created in the image of God as was the man. You can prove from Holy Writ that Holy Spirit Mother, counterpart of Father God, is the heavenly Model for the wife, mother, and woman on earth.

Now we are going to look at the biblical approach to marriage and family. Please take a moment to read Ephesians 5:15-33. It is important that I first share with you the fact that in the original Bible manuscript, the phrase "wives submit" in verse 22 was not present. Some men, later, inserted this word. Paul wrote lengthy sentences, which some transcribers and translators thought needed to be divided up into shorter sentences for clarity. So the word "submit" was placed after the word "wives" by these people. Verses 21 and 22 are really of the same sentence. It is in the context of husbands and wives submitting to one another that verse 22 was written.

So in the setting of a wife submitting to her husband, the husband also submits to his wife. In Christ there is perfect equality as He brings the family back to its original state of godliness before sin. During the time Paul wrote this letter to the believers at Ephesus, he husband in the family was in complete control of his household. The wife and children and servants had no voice and no autonomy whatsoever. Paul upsets this sinful tradition by now commanding that there has to be mutual submission for those who profess Christianity.

Here Paul does not command the wives to submit to their husband in order to let the husband rule over the wife. He is speaking of a mutual attitude of the husband and the wife toward each other and of them together being submitted to Christ. But then Paul goes on to give husbands five other commands of responsibility to his wife.

In verse 33, Paul tells the husband that he must so love his wife like he loves himself *so that* the wife will respect him. The original Greek writing that means *in order that* the wife respects her husband was changed to make it a command for the wife to respect her husband. This is incorrect. What Paul is saying is that the husband will earn respect when he actively loves and treats his wife as his equal and provide for her like Christ provides for the Church.

Can you imagine what the men of his day thought of him and the teachings he presented to the church from God? What had been going on for thousands of years and accepted by most, is now being challenged by this apostle of God. Patriarchal sinful tradition was put on notice by the progressive preacher Paul. If the Christian church had followed this godly, God-ordained formula for the family, this world would not be in the bad shape it is in at the present time. When will we learn?

But even if we were to go along with the insertion of this "submit yourselves to your own husband" as it is now, let us look at it with godly insight:

Ephesians 5:22. "Wives, submit yourselves unto your own husbands, as unto the Lord."

Colossians 3:18. "Wives, submit yourselves unto your own husbands, as it is fit in the Lord." According to the Greek Dictionary of the New Testament in the *Strong's Exhaustive Concordance of the Bible,* page 260, the word *submit* originates from the Greek *hupotage.* This was originally a Greek military term that means to arrange as in troop divisions under the command of a leader. But in non-military use it means a voluntary attitude of giving in, cooperating, and assuming responsibility. *Submit* also means to yield, to allow, to permit, to give way. And if you read the texts that follow the command for the wives to submit, you will then understand to whom, to what, and why they are to submit. So let us read the verses that follow.

Ephesians 5:23-28. "For the husband is the head of the wife (it does not say that *man* is the head of the woman, but that *a husband* is the head of the wife), even as Christ is the head of the church: and he is the savior (preserver and sustainer) of the body. Therefore as the church is subject unto Christ, so let the wives be to their own husbands in everything. Husbands, love your wives, even as Christ also loved the church, and gave himself for it; …So ought men to love their wives as their own bodies. He that loveth his wife loveth himself. For no man ever hated his own flesh; but nourisheth and cherisheth it, even as the Lord the church."

Colossians 3:19. "Husbands, love your wives and be not bitter against them."

So we see here that after each verse concerning the wife's submission follows the verse concerning the husband's love, the reason for submission. If we then would apply the accurate working definition of *submission*, we can readily see to whom, to what and why a wife is to submit. This is the way we would then understand the spirit of the texts:

Paraphrase: Wife permit, allow, give way, yield, subject yourself to your husband's active love for you. This love is the same love that Jesus has for His own bride, the church. Jesus loved the church so much that He gave everything He had for her, even His own life. Everything He did, He did it for His bride. He led her by example. He served her and declared that the leader is the servant of all. He empowers her, provides for her every need in abundance and protects her. So allow, permit, give way, yield, and subject yourself to this same kind of royal treatment. Your husband is your provider, servant-partner and friend. Respect him as such; and receive him as such.

The wife has to have that love in order to submit to it, of course. Without the active love of the husband that Paul commands of the husband, there is nothing to which the wife can submit. She is to submit to the equality of status and to the provision of the husband, because these are the privileges that he too enjoys. And the husband is to love his wife exactly the way he loves himself. Without a life committed to active love, humility cannot exist in that life. And without humility, unity cannot exist within the family. This goes directly against the very foundation of the patriarchal establishment, which is based on the pridefulness of the male ego.

Remember what Jesus told His church before His crucifixion. He said to His own bride in John 15:15, "I call you not servants…but I have called you friends." So when we apply this attitudinal principle to the marriage unit, we see that the bride is not the servant. The servant is the husband. He is the source of provision for his family. A godly husband treats his bride the way Jesus treats His bride, the church. Everything Jesus did, He did for his bride. And He says that the husband is the head of the wife as Jesus is the head of the church. Jesus, as Head, meaning source and origin, gave his very life for the benefit of His bride. Jesus even became obedient unto death, even the death of the cross, for his bride. The word head has taken on a different meaning since being recorded in the Bible. As we learned earlier, headship, leadership and rulership impose the status and position of a servant, according to the God's Word. And that is exactly what Jesus Christ modeled when He was on earth.

What a wonderful blessing for all women who decide to marry. However, the word *submit* has been misrepresented. It has been taken by some and presented as something other than what God intended. God is orderly, fair, compassionate and loving. When women, who are naturally independent, as seen in their early childhood development and behavior, permit someone to actively provide and love them in the godly manner, they will experience the blessing in which God planned for them to have. They are to make themselves the object of their husbands' love and service. And when husbands take the initiative to be good providers, protectors, service-oriented partners in their own family, without becoming bitter or weary in well-doing, then they too will experience the joy that Jesus experiences as Head of the church. We as Christians respect and love Christ because He first loved us. He does not demand respect; He earned it.

Also, it is important to point out here that the word "head" as read in verse 23 "For the husband is the head of the wife" is the Greek word *kephale.* This word means source and origin. Since a rib was taken out of man at creation for the forming of woman, the man was the source of bone God used to create the woman. Therefore, the male-man is the giver, and the female-man is the receiver in the family unit. We can see this even in the physical make up of the female and male reproductive organs. Additionally, the husband is the giver, source and origin for the care and love of his wife. Jesus Christ is the source and origin of the church. And the God family, with Father God and Holy Spirit Mother God, is the source of Christ to us because they are the Ones that sent Him here. Christ is God. Christ, the Son of God, eternally and equally shares deity in the Trinity, Elohim (see 1 John 5:7 and Philippians 2:6). I believe that if we understand the texts about marriage in this way, which benefits both spouses, our world would be much better in every way.

The traditional way we have viewed the family structure is exactly the opposite of the truth of God in Christ.

Husbands should take time and put forth effort to seriously study Jesus' life principles in caring for His bride, the church. Then they would know how to treat and care for their wife. The wife must receive and experience that love to which she will submit. Again, respect is something earned. One must submit himself and serve his way into leadership. Then let us not overlook the text that commands us all to "submit one to another," Ephesians 5:21. The traditional way we have viewed the family structure is exactly the opposite of the truth of God in Christ.

You see, Satan's main focus since Eden has been to divide and war against the family, because it was created to look like and to operate like God, whom Satan hates. So we find that because of the lie that women cause men to sin, during Jesus' time on earth, men were not permitted to converse with or even touch a woman in public, as indicated earlier. But Jesus conversed with and touched women in public. He taught women in the circle of discipleship. In 1 Corinthians 15:45 Jesus is called the "last Adam." In other words, He came to undo what Adam had done and to do what had Adam failed to do. Jesus Christ of Nazareth is an awesome man. He is our awesome God.

Satan well understands that the greatest asset a person can have is that of a spouse. He very well knows that if husbands and wives could just experience the wonders of a godly marriage his kingdom would be defeated very quickly. Satan's greatest weapon against humankind is the weapon of ignorance. As long as people believe Satan's lies and follow his suggestions in man-woman, male-female interactions, he wins.

Any husband who puts himself first and above his wife as the head, ruler and lord in the traditionally sinful way; and without the service aspect in action and humility, is not at all following Jesus' example and will have to answer to God soon in the Judgment. Any husband who takes all the credit for good outcomes and delegates all blame to his wife for bad outcomes is not a good husband. We must accept all of Jesus, or we receive none of Jesus. It is just that simple.

Allow me to show another example of the wife on earth shadowing the heavenly Wife—Holy Spirit Mother. In Proverbs 8:35 wisdom personified is speaking: "For whoso findeth me findeth life, and shall obtain favour of the Lord." As we have learned, the Holy Spirit is the Spirit of wisdom. And the human female is made in the image and likeness of Holy Spirit Mother. In the book of Proverbs wisdom is always called "she" just as the Hebrew word for *wisdom* is a feminine word. With this in mind let us now compare this text with Proverbs 18:22, where the Bible is addressing the male regarding the female saying, "Whoso findeth a wife findeth a good thing, and obtaineth favour of the Lord." So here we see the same truth said of the Holy Spirit, the Spirit of wisdom is also said of the female and wife on earth. "Thy will be done on earth, as it is in heaven." A good man will pursue both the wisdom of the Spirit and a good wife. An enlightened man will understand that there is a connection between his own wife and the Holy Spirit, because his wife was created to reflect the image and likeness of the Holy Spirit. And when he has both, God's favor will rest on him. When a man is filled with the Holy Spirit and becomes as one flesh with a good wife, he is assured of God's blessing and favor. This is a biblical promise.

An enlightened man will understand that there is a connection between his own wife and the Holy Spirit, because his wife was created to reflect the image and likeness of the Holy Spirit. And when he has both, God's favor will rest on him.

Before sin, Adam-man stated, "Therefore shall a man leave his father and mother, and shall cleave unto his wife" (Genesis 2:24). The word, *cleave,* means to actively pursue, to connect with and to ensure a strong bond of unity. But after sin entered the family, this standard for the man was abandoned and replaced with the woman's overflowing emotion leading to a different standard, "thy desire shall be to thy husband, and he shall rule over thee" (Genesis 3:16). The standard before sin is the one in which the family would experience heaven on earth. The latter standard has not benefited gender and family relationships at all. Instead it leads to hell on earth. This latter standard has proven to be the greatest cause of pain, abuse, confusion and strife. Our goal should be to move forward until we return to primitive godliness, the circle of relational restoration and perfection. This is the place of perfect peace, *shalom*, where there is nothing missing and nothing broken.

Now, let us move on. In the counsel for wives to submit is found the reasons and blessings for which they are to submit. And in this same counsel is the love-in-action command that is given to the husband. It is the exact formula of provision that Jesus Christ carries out for His wife, the church. Let's look at this magical marriage message housed in the word *submit*:

S—Safety. Jesus said, "I will build my church (bride of Christ). And the gates of hell will not prevail against it" (Matthew 16:18). "When the enemy shall come in like a flood, the Spirit of the Lord will lift up a standard against him" (Isaiah 59:19). The husband patterns Jesus in ensuring his wife's safety, both the physical, emotional, and spiritual. He makes arrangements for his family's total safekeeping. He ensures his wife's emotional protection by honoring her and by not allowing outside influences to dishonor her or their marriage. Along with his wife, he is to be the initiator of spiritual direction for the family. And he is to keep out all attitudes and influences that will tear down the moral fabric of his home, such as pornography, unwholesome television shows, unwholesome music, abuse, infidelity, partnership inequity as well as all outsiders who undermine the godly values that we have studied.

U—Unity. Jesus said, "At that day ye shall know that I am in my Father, and ye in me, and I in you" (John 14:20; 17:21-23). Just as Jesus Christ is the initiator and connector for humankind into divine union with our God family, so the husband initiates and maintains a good connection between all members of the family. Jesus said to His disciples, "By this shall all men know that ye are my disciples, if ye have love one to another" (John 13:35). A wise man understands that disunity will breed mutiny. "A house divided against itself shall not stand" (Matthew 12:25). Where there is inequity there cannot be unity. Toleration may exist, but not unity and peace. I believe this to be the primary and underlying reason for divorce and domestic turmoil. Fifty percent of marriages in the United States of America end in divorce. It is because we do not approach marriage in the way of God's plan for such institution. Instead, we approach marriage and other relationships in the way of sinful tradition.

B—Blessing. It is the duty and privilege of the husband to pronounce blessing over his wife, the works of her hands, and over the family. This began with God, the Father's pronouncing blessing over the Holy Spirit's work at the end of creation week, saying, "Behold it is very good." It is interesting to note that an ancient Jewish tradition that still exists today is one in which the husband gathers the family on Friday evening (the end of the work week) and ushers in the Sabbath rest by pronouncing blessings over his wife first and then over each child. The husband praises his wife for the good works she has done during the week. Proverbs 31 records that the wonderful husband of the virtuous woman also did this. He praised her not only in private but also at the city gates. No wonder this woman was so successful and lived in abundance emotionally, relationally and financially. She had a great husband who supported her and actively loved her with the Christ kind of love.

M—Money. "It is your Father's good pleasure to give you the kingdom" (Luke 12:32). "And I will give unto thee the keys of the kingdom of heaven" (Matthew 16:19). "The Lord thy God giveth thee power to get wealth" (Deuteronomy 8:18). "But if any provide not for his own, and specially for those of his own house, he hath denied the faith, and is worse than an infidel" (1 Timothy 5:8). Temporal provision for the wife and family is the duty and privilege of the husband. A man is to do what is needed in order to take care of his family. If he is not ready to adequately and consistently provide for a family, he is not ready for marriage. The Bible says that a husband should leave his parents and cleave to his wife, as mentioned earlier. This means among other things that he should not be dependent on his parents to provide for his needs and for his family's needs. And then, on the other hand, we find that there are some men who require their wives to abandon their very young children in order to go to work and help him make money to take care of the family. I believe that a capable husband allows and encourages his wife to nurture their own young children. When the children are older, the wife can then choose to go outside of the home and work. But regardless, a family's budget should not be based on the income of the wife. This is my own personal opinion that was actually taught to me by my husband. And this is not to say that her income cannot be used to pay bills. What it means is that the husband should be well able to take care of his family financially, such that the wife's income, no matter how large it may be, is more like a continual bonus. And this makes sense because in a household budget, if your income exceeds your expenses, you will be a prosperous family and have more to plant into the kingdom of God. And that is good news in itself.

I— Initiative. A husband is to initiate goodness and positivism into his wife's life. Genesis 1:1-3 paraphrased: In the beginning the God family created the heaven and the earth. Holy Spirit Mother moved upon the face of the waters. And then Father God said, "Let there be light!" And there was light. Father God, through speaking words of active love, initiated goodness to combine with the efforts of Holy Spirit Mother in the creation process.

As we have discovered in the Scriptures, Holy Spirit Mother was the initiating force in creation. She was Adam-woman's model and is also the model for today's woman.

T—Treatment. A husband is to treat his wife with tenderness and respect. This behavior is a learned behavior. Usually a son observes and learns from his father, or other males, how a wife and a woman should be treated. During courtship a woman dating a man should carefully notice how this man treats his mother, his sister, and females that he is not courting. Because this same behavior toward them will be turned to the wife after their honeymoon is over. Watch carefully, and be wise. Also let me add here that if a husband allows another man to "rule over" his wife, put her down in any way, or even to "provide" for her, this husband is not protecting his wife. A wife has one marriage "head." If another man comes and takes on this role, the husband is not being a responsible spouse. No man has a right or responsibility to act as "head" of another man's wife. Such a man needs to be swiftly and definitively corrected. If the husband is not up to the task of correcting such a man, the wife should not hesitate to do so.

After sin entered our existence, God told Adam that the ground was cursed. But through the knowledge God later supplied, man has been able to overcome the effects of a cursed ground. So now by making and using tools, irrigation techniques, machines, and proper timing, man has basically overcome this curse. But cursed ground also means the general workforce system. God has provided principles in His Word to help the believer overcome obstacles to success in every area of life. God caused the childbearing process to be a painful one for the mother. But later, He taught us how to overcome this effect of sin as well. Through medical advances and various techniques, this kind of pain and suffering has been minimized and is even non-existent in many cases. Many medical advances have been made through female researchers. There is a great need for female professionals in every area of human existence. I appeal to every woman to consider advancing in education. The world is waiting for you to help solve its problems!

God had also prophesied, not commanded, that the husband would rule over his wife. The misinterpretation of this prophecy, taken as a command, has caused so many problems and so much pain and tension in human relations as a whole. And so God sent Jesus Christ to set the record straight. Jesus Himself said that He came to "set at liberty them that are bruised" (Luke 4:18). And in the Garden of Eden, the serpent did indeed bruise the woman. Her influence, her rightful position, her relationship to God, her relationship to her husband and to the male gender were bruised. And just as he bruised her, so he bruised the "Seed of the woman," Jesus Christ. But the Seed crushed the serpent's head. He brought defeat to the kingdom of darkness. Jesus is the Light of the world! Because of victory wrought by Jesus, the "last Adam" we find that in Christ "there is neither male nor female" (Galatians 3:28). So instead of a husband ruling over his wife in the way of sinful tradition, the husband now realizes that a "ruler" is a servant with heavy responsibility for another person. There is a BIG difference here, my friends. Those of us who profess to be Christians must then live and interact with one another in the same manner and spirit that Jesus did when He was here on earth. Jesus came to restore the woman back to the position within the family structure and on earth in general that she had before sin entered the world. This is the place of absolute equality to that of the man and her husband. Through the blood of Jesus, men and women can begin again. They are free from the curse of sin according to God's word. And men and women whom the Son has set free are free indeed.

You can now see this concept of "wives submit to your own husband" is wonderful. It simply means that wives should allow, permit and give way to benefits from the husband, who is the partner-provider-servant, source and origin of active love. All that a husband does should be done for God and for his wife. All that he has should be for God and for his wife. This is the same relationship that Christ has with His Father and His bride-church.

All that a husband does should be done for God and for his wife. All that he has should be for God and for his wife. This is the same relationship that Christ has with His Father and His bride-church.

Welcome this. It's great! What a wonderful gift of **s**afety, **u**nity, **b**lessing, **m**oney, **i**nitiative, and **t**ender treatment. God is a God of purity and compassion. And He wants us to know His will concerning family. Our model family is God. In the light of God's truth women should not mourn for being women. They should celebrate that they are women. We all need to celebrate our differences. We were made with certain characteristic attributes as men and women. The God family modeled different roles for husbands and wives. We all need to study for ourselves the word and will of the Lord. We all contribute to the completeness of human existence. Our world could not exist without both the male and the female. God made it this way. Families on earth are to represent and reflect the image and likeness of the God family. In unity our diversity produces fruitfulness.

Abundant life is found where the wholeness of the earthly family reflects the holiness of the God family. "Thy will be done on earth as it is in heaven."

Abundant life is found where the wholeness of the earthly family reflects the holiness of the God family. "Thy will be done on earth, as it is in heaven."

Chapter Twelve

Family of Mine

Having made the choice to unite with Maurice Cates, I took on an additional life role, wife to my husband. So, although I am still myself, I have taken on someone and something more. Yet my wife status does not undo, redo, nor forfeit my original state. It adds to it. Therefore, I have additional responsibilities as a wife; and I have additional help as a wife. My husband and I partner through a life covenant in order to become bigger and better (Ecclesiastes 4:9-12) and to nurture companionship that would cradle us for the rest of our life. We married in order to bless one another in every conceivable way and not for one to rule over the other in the traditional—and wrong—meaning of *married.* My husband is not the head of me as an individual. Jesus Christ is the Head of me—all of me. My husband is the head of my position in the family as wife. The Bible says that the husband is head of the wife, as we have studied in the previous chapter. I am more than a wife. I have other positions, responsibilities and life activities besides being a wife. Therefore, my husband is not the head of these other positions. He is not the source and origin of the person that I continue to be, before I knew him. He is the source, reason and origin of my wife life. Without a husband, I could not be a wife.

Maurice and I were doing exceptionally well before we met. We were confident and comfortable in life before knowing that the other existed. After we married we continued working hard and enjoyed it. We enjoyed each other very much, and still do. Maurice is the Chief of Service of Orthopedic Surgery and a member of the Board of Directors where he works. I was a member of a very successful physicians' group as well as an Executive Officer on the Board of Directors. Maurice and I had a full life together as well as individually. We decided some years later to have children.

I returned to work five weeks after giving birth to our first child. Our in-home childcare expectations were not met. My heart ached for our child, but it never occurred to me to stop working and take care of my own offspring. My baby and I did not see one another very much. Only after Maurice talked to me about the idea of my staying home for a while did a different level of maternal yearning awaken within my spirit. Although caring for the sick and injured in a very busy emergency department, a very fulfilling responsibility to me, I also started to feel such a longing in my heart for my baby. Yet I could not see myself without this very active and fulfilling career.

Then one evening Maurice told me that he would put his career on hold to stay home and care for our family. He also told me that he thought I would do a better job at caring for the family in the home setting. His message of compassion and willing sacrifice pierced my soul. I was somewhat ashamed that I, the mother, found it hard to give up my career for our family. Then I decided to follow his servant-leadership attitude and stay home with our child. We soon decided to complete our family while I was working at home.

However, the transition was almost unbearable. I can recall sitting on the kitchen floor many a time, crying and crying and crying. I found it to be incredibly difficult to go from opening up a trauma victim's chest to repair a gunshot wounded heart, to opening up a jar of baby food. To move from giving intravenous injections to stop a patient's seizure activity, to giving pacifiers to stop my child's whining was a big change. From sitting in high-powered board meetings making corporate decisions, to sitting in a rocking chair making bedtime story selections, was a challenge. From washing debris out of body wounds, to washing dishes and diapers and windows and walls was indeed a culture shock. And to go from receiving field calls of paramedics bringing patients for medical care, to receiving calls from colleagues and friends inquiring about my decision to put my career on hold, sent me into a tailspin. Then to top all this off, some church members and especially certain church leaders overtly implied that my working at home with the family was a big step downward. And by their behavior, they showed me that a woman temporarily on leave from her career for the welfare of the family unit is not due the same respect given to a man on permanent leave from his career as a retiree. What an affront to the high value of motherhood and to the family unit, which God created.

Since I didn't know how to handle these changes properly, and since I had not gathered enough biblical knowledge of my standing in Christ as both a devoted mother and wife and as a professional woman of God, I slipped into sub-clinical depression. Yes, I was still active in the church and doing much more than any mother with suckling infants and toddlers should do. Yes, I was a good mother, caring quite well for our children, home and family. But my children and husband did not know just how I really felt. I was actually like a dead woman on the inside.

But God is faithful. Jesus Christ is indeed the "resurrection and the life." He supernaturally delivered me from this simmering type of depression that eventually escalated into desperation. Very early one morning as I prepared for my suicide, Satan appeared and assured me that this was the best thing to do. And as I embraced the prospect of the "peace" of death, an unseen Being audibly called me by name. Of course I immediately looked in the direction of the sound. When I turned back around, Satan the liar was gone. This voice said that the enemy of souls had "asked" for me but that Jesus, my elder Brother, was praying for me. Then I was told, with a sense of urgency, to get up and go pray for myself. I did. And during the time of prostration in prayer and receiving comfort, God revealed his thoughts to me concerning my children and our family unit. Our conversation and my supernatural emotional and spiritual transition lasted for about eight hours. After documenting the promises, I continue tracking the process, the progress and the provisions surrounding these promises God gave me. During the time that I was prostrate on the floor of my library, enveloped in a bright sheet of light that was pure and heavy, God gave me steps to take for complete healing from that horrible depression. As I followed these instructions day by day, I was healed. And a complete health education system was put into place to share with others. God told me to give myself a CHECK UP, a lifestyle acronym to enhance health, happiness and wholeness. From this process National CHECK UP, Inc. was created.

Later that same morning, when my youngest child (eighteen months old at that time) woke up, he looked deeply into my swollen eyes and called me "Mommy Beautiful." He had never used that term nor the word *beautiful* before. So I new that this was God's confirmation through my baby. And ever since that morning of the year 2000, all my children continue to call me, Mommy Beautiful.

So with three children, a supportive and loving husband, the personal promises of God to me, God's image of who I am down-loaded into my spirit, the living Word of God to guide my walk through life, the presence, power and ministry of Holy Spirit Mother with Her daily fresh anointing, the blood of Jesus Christ for cleansing and protection, and my daily CHECK UP, I can say that joy of the Lord is my strength. God has made all grace abound to me, so that in all things at all times, having all I need, I will abound in every good work, according to 2 Corinthians 9:8.

Minister Evelyn Ross, a mighty woman of God, church leader and health care worker, whom I have never worked with, had a vision about me three days after my conversation with God. I had told no one about that experience—not even Maurice—but she told me the exact words and promises that God had spoken. This was another confirmation God sent to me. There have been many con-firmation experiences since that time. And for the next seven months, such confirmations came almost daily.

One of the several things God told me was that if I would care for his little children like I was doing but with a godly perspective, He would take special care of me and would "restore" my years in due season. During the time away from my career and after that transition experience, God has led me into a deep study of His holy, living word. He gives me fresh Bread and living Water every single morning. The Bible, God's Word, is my book of magic and is indeed alive. It sharpens my mind, washes and renews it every day.

It teaches me just how God thinks and what He thinks of me. It literally strengthens my physical body and relaxes me. It has restored my self-esteem. Time alone with God early in the morning makes the rest of day run with efficiency. There have been so many wonderful miracles in my life. When I think of any one of them, I can't help but to praise the Lord with shouts of praise and tearful gratitude. I love God so much. And I do trust Him completely. God is better than good. He is absolutely awesome. All praise, honor and glory belong to Him. I have learned that the very best habit any person can develop is to "seek ye first the kingdom of God, and His righteousness" through personal Bible study, prayer, praise and worship as the first activities of the day.

God is Faithful

During the time away from my career, in 2002, the Emergency Medicine Board Recertification examination became due, which must be taken every 10 years. But having a very hectic schedule of home schooling our three children, caring for the home, heading our family ministries activities, producing my debut music CD, writing this book, composing songs and several other pressing projects, I did not have much time to study. One morning, Holy Spirit Mother taught me a new way to study. The two years of study-time I needed to have done, but had not, was actually done in the two months before the exam. Many physicians take about two years to get through the volume of information needed to pass the exam. And I had planned to do the same, especially since I had not been active in my career for a while. This study technique, given to me by God, is a unique and revolutionary formula that would be such an asset for Christian students. I believe that God does not depend on a person's ability, but rather on a person's humility and availability.

Just as a testimony, and certainly not for bragging purposes at all, I can tell you that God showed strong in my life during this study and testing process. He allowed and blessed me to score even higher than I had ten years before when working in the emergency room, studying hard and with no children. Not only on that particular exam, but also on two other clinical recertification exams, I scored 100% each time. God indeed came through in a big way thrice. I share the formula for this study and test-taking technique with churches, schools, groups and individuals wanting to operate in the realm of excellence.

God is no respecter of persons. His mercy extends to all who will receive it. God's goodness and power are available to those who would dare to plug in and receive.

God is no respecter of persons. His mercy extends to all who will receive it. God's goodness and power are available to those who would dare to plug in and receive.

God made all believers to be a blessed people. We are "blessed in the city and blessed in the field" (Deuteronomy 28:3). Blessings shall overtake us.

He made us to be a righteous people. And we are the "righteousness of God in [Jesus]" (2 Corinthians 5:21).

He made us all to be a reflection of His image and His likeness. And we are just that, human beings who resemble God in form and in likeness (Genesis 1:27).

He made us to "have life, and have it more abundantly" (John 10:10). We just need to choose that life, so that it will be well with us and with our children.

He made us to have perfect peace. And we do have perfect peace with our eyes stayed on God, and God alone (Isaiah 26:3).

Lead on, Little Children

The Bible says in Isaiah 40: 11, that God gently leads those with young children. From experience I can tell you that this is so true. Because of the faithfulness of God and the manliness of my best friend and husband, I have not "missed a beat" in any way. In many ways my life has been far more fruitful during the several years working at home than when I was working outside of the home. "Let the redeemed of the Lord say so" (Psalms 107:2).

What I believed to be the worst chapter of my life, working at home with our children, has actually been the very best for me, next to God and Maurice. My children are adorable, loving, Holy Spirit-filled, wonderful, brilliant, happy and beautiful children. God has used them on many occasions to prophesy over my life and over my day. They have witnessed many wonderful miracles in their short lifetime. They understand deep things of God and are devoted to God. They are pure in heart and have taught me so much. I have given them over to God and consecrate them to the Lord every morning. By the laying on of hands and speaking blessings over them and teaching them the Word of the Lord, God abides in them and they in Him. You should hear these babies speak. They are dynamic public speakers! They have ministered to many public officials, congressmen, senators, diplomats, educators, various professional groups, artistic luminaries, as well as at churches, schools, concerts, galas and other functions. They are a source of encouragement and inspiration to many thousands of people all over the United States and abroad. God has spoken to each of them directly. They know His voice. I praise God every single day for each one of them. He knew just what we needed. Blessed is the name of the Lord.

As an aside, our children have never been spanked. The rod of discipline does not have to be a wooden stick or a leather strap. Perhaps our method of discipline will not work for all families. And I am not advocating a "do not touch" approach to parenting. Our children only recently learned about the concept of "spanking" through a friend. They were fascinated. When you spend time with your children and they learn to really trust in what you, the parents say, mostly by parental actions in consistency and lifestyle, I believe that physical discipline can be kept to the bare minimum. And concerning home schooling and childhood development, I believe that godly parents, and not other children, should socialize our children.

I have learned so much about God because of these precious ones in my life; and have learned so much about the way God thinks and the way He operates just from this little family He has given me. There is nothing more important to me than my God family and my Cates family. The blood of Jesus Christ, the spotless Lamb of God, is applied to my home and family members every morning, by the laying on of hands and confessing our belief in Jesus Christ as Lord. We plead the blood. After His blood is applied by faith and confession, then God applies fresh oil, a fresh anointing of enabling grace by Holy Spirit Mother.

Let me share just one small example of many, many events that have occurred in our home. My children began to speak in tongues without my telling them of this concept. One afternoon, our older son, Maurice II, age 6, lay prostrate on the bedroom floor. The other two children were running in and out of the room laughing and saying, "Maurdy is talking funny!" So I went to see what they were talking about. Upon entering the room, I heard him praying in a language I could not recognize. After he was finished, about 10 minutes later, I asked him what was he doing. He said, "O, Mommy, I was just talking to God." I said, "But we couldn't understand your words, son." Then he said, "Well God understands, because I was talking to Him. And Satan can't understand my prayer, Mommy." I then began to share with them my limited understanding of this biblical subject, which I had only read about during personal Bible study.

I had been secretly praying for the ability to speak in tongues. No one knew about it at all. It was my secret. I had read about it in the Bible, but wasn't sure if this was something that could or even should really be done. Please read a few of the Bible texts on this type of prayer (Acts 2:4; 10:45, 46; 19:6; 1 Corinthians 12:10 and 14:18, 22). A few nights later before going to sleep, I asked God to open my spirit like that of a little child and allow me to pray in the Spirit someday as a prayer language to build up my "most holy faith" (Jude 20). That night, as I entered into a different kind of dream realm, similar to the ones I have had during depositions of revelation knowledge, I actually dreamed that I was fervently praying for the manifestation of having been baptized in the Holy Spirit.

Then in the dream I began to speak in tongues. This went on, seemingly, for a long time.

As I came out of the dream, woke up, opened my eyes and sat up in bed, I was still speaking in a prayer language unto the Lord. Then, putting my hand over my mouth so as not to awaken my husband, I quickly jumped out of bed and raced to the library and praised God for this wonderful miracle! The experience was awesome. My spirit was free and I was perfectly at peace. This event ushered in a higher level of spiritual awareness, insight and miracles in my life. God is so very good. My children and I do continue praying in the Spirit. Yes, "And a little child shall lead them" (Isaiah 11:6).

Of course there are different types of prayers. Praying in tongues is only one of them. A person can pray in tongues without really praying in the Spirit. And a person can pray in the Spirit without praying in tongues. Everyone does not believe in nor desire to pray in tongues, but I do. And God allows me to do so. God shows me everyday that He is trustworthy. And certainly, I do trust Him completely, from victory unto victory, from strength to strength, from glory to glory!

We should get a vision from God concerning our future, our purpose, and our rightful position on this earth. If you do not have one, ask Him to give you one. "Where there is no vision, the people perish" (Proverbs 29:18). When you have and yield to the vision of God for your life, you become unstoppable, because God watches over His word and performs His purposes.

Here is a writing that was given to me by the Holy Spirit soon after the conversation we had, the morning I was delivered from despair. It is dedicated to the time I have been home with our children. And I dedicate it to those of you who have put your own dreams and plans on hold to nurture others. Remember that God always repays at least double for your trouble. The sacrifices you make are only for a season, but the resulting blessing to others and to yourself will last for eternity.

This is my silent time:
A time for introspecting and interceding.
A time for sacrificing and supporting.
A time for nurturing and educating.
A time for uplifting and outreaching.

This is my silent time:
A time for reorganizing and reprioritizing.
A time for relearning and reinforcing.
A time for regrouping and recapturing.
A time for returning and rebuilding.

This is my silent time:
A time for recognizing and revealing
A time for responding and relenting
A time for releasing and recovering
A time for reconciling and rectifying

Yes indeed, this is my silent time,
A time for repenting and rejoicing.
This is my time for
Rebirth and Restoration!

Walesia Robinson Cates

Family Adoption

And now dear reader, if you have never accepted Jesus Christ as your best Friend, Savior, elder Brother, and Redeemer or if you have distanced yourself from the relationship you used to have with Him and you want to return, I invite you to do so right now. Joining yourself with Jesus is the very best thing you could ever do for yourself. He will come into your life and give you new meaning, a new mind, a new attitude, and a renewed spirit. He will bear your burdens for you. He will set you free and teach you how to operate His Holy Word for abundant life. You will learn that He is faithful and trustworthy. Jesus Christ will change your life.

Let's pray audibly: Heavenly Father, because of Your Son, Jesus, I can come to the throne of grace. I believe that Jesus is the Son of God, that He died for my sins and that the Spirit of God raised Him from the dead. I believe in You and receive You into my life right now. Knowing that You are faithful to forgive, I confess my sins and receive cleansing from all unrighteousness. Take complete control of my life, through the presence, power and ministry of Holy Spirit Mother and lead me in the path of right standing before God. Now I am a child of God. Jesus is my elder Brother. And I am willing to mature into the full authority of sonship/daughtership. Thank You for Your love. In the name of Jesus Christ, amen.

If you prayed this prayer audibly and sincerely, you have certainly been forgiven of your sins and are now a saved member in God's family. You have become the righteousness of God because of Jesus Christ. He is your triune connection. God's Spirit is in you. Glory to God in the highest; and peace, goodwill to you. Learn more about Jesus and your God family by uniting with a Bible teaching, truth living, commandment keeping, church family. Tell others about your salvation. Allow Jesus to lead and to keep you in the path of righteousness. Because this is the same path where "blessings shall overtake thee" (Deuteronomy 28:2). Watch what God does in your life from now on. Stay connected with the Ones who love you: Father God, Son of God and Holy Spirit Mother God. They are the Holy Family, Creator of the universe, your true Source and Origin.

And lastly, children of God, my sisters and brothers, you need to know that I love you and care about your well-being. I am praying for you, that you will enjoy the wonderful love of God and the abundant life that Jesus came to give you. You are just surrounded by so much love! You can only love yourself when you understand and believe in the unconditional love God has for you. God has "plans to prosper you, plans to give you hope and a future" (Jeremiah 29:11 NIV).

I hope and pray that this book has been a blessing to you. Do not look back. Just continue to go forward in the strength of God. Open up your spirit and let your Holy Spirit Mother come in, along with your Father and Brother. We stand in agreement for family unity, as members of the Most High God family, the Trinity. And in the name of Jesus Christ, I declare it done. Amen!

Family Pledge

When you are ready, please take this family oath with me:

We are family soldiers in the army of the Lord,
Fighting the good fight of faith,
Proclaiming "victory in Jesus!"

We are family workers in our fields,
Studying, achieving, laboring, creating,
Putting our shoulders to the plow as we
Nurture and provide for those whom
God has given to us.

We are family believers of what is true,
And pure, and noble and of good report, and
Worthy of our thought, our time, our energy.

We are kindred by blood, by marriage,
By life experiences, by human need,
By spiritual need, by dreams,
By hopes, and expectations.
We take the oath to the keeping of our family circle.

We are family, understanding the value of family;
And will forever abide herein.
May the Holy Spirit of God forever abide in each of us.
And all of the family shall say together, Amen!

Walesia Robinson Cates

Biography

Dr. Walesia Robinson Cates was born in Orlando, Florida. Through the guidance of the Holy Spirit and her parents, she exhibited uniqueness at a very early age. During spring and summer vacation time, young Walesia became an accomplished horticulturist while farming with her mother. She developed skills of breaking up ground, cultivating soil, planting seed, harvesting large crops of many different vegetables, shucking corn, shelling peas, banking potatoes, picking okra and canning freshly harvested produce. If not farming, she was working as a housekeeper and caretaker of new-borns, infants and children. If she was not doing either of these, she was working as a literature evangelist, inspirational vocalist and a winner of souls to God's kingdom, while earning scholarship funds for high school and college tuition. Walesia also learned the power of fasting and praying since early childhood. She learned how to be a pray-er of faith very early in life.

She has served her church and community as a soloist both locally, throughout the continental U.S and abroad, including the Caribbean and Canada. She has served the *Breath of Life* telecast as solo vocalist, airing in countries around the world. She served on the Oakwood College Church Board in youth leadership, as well as on the Church Hostess Committee during her high school and college years. Walesia served as health presenter for the Youth Department during Vacation Bible School sessions at the Oakwood College Church. She continues to be active in the church community at large, in different denominations, as health presenter, Bible studies presenter, Women's Ministries speaker, musical vocalist and hospitality minister.

Walesia exhibited an unwavering resolve for excellence throughout her academic career, graduating as Valedictorian from Oakwood Junior Academy as well as Oakwood Christian Academy four years later and was featured in *Who's Who in High Schools of America.* Her successes were not limited to academics. Walesia was also well known for her accomplishments in track and field competitions during all four years of high school. She was *Miss Oakwood Academy 1977.* During college years, she was a member of the Oakwood College Recruitment Team, was a recipient of the UNCF Scholarship Award, served as music coordinator for the United Student Movement, was featured in *Who's Who in Colleges and Universities of America* and was recognized as *"Outstanding Young Woman of America 1981."*

She graduated Magna Cum Laude from Oakwood College with a Bachelor of Arts degree in Biology. Then after graduating from University of Alabama at Birmingham School of Medicine, she moved to Washington, DC, accepting a position in the Emergency Medicine Residency Program at Howard University Hospital.

And while at Howard University Hospital she met the young man of her dream, Maurice Cates, M.D., an Orthopaedic surgeon. They developed and nurtured a wonderful friendship and entered into covenant relationship of marriage two years later. She settled with her beloved husband in the Washington D.C. metropolitan area.

After completing the Emergency Medicine program, Dr. Cates became the first African-American female to join the prestigious Southeast Emergency Physicians Group in Washington, D.C. There, she became a senior partner, a member of the Board of Directors, and Executive Secretary of the Board. After several years of service and leadership there, she utilized her entrepreneurial skills to co-found an Emergency Medicine physicians group practice in Southern Maryland.

Dr. Cates has also been active in the community. She served as Medical Officer for the Mayoral Medical Council during the 1993 Presidential Inauguration, served on the Emergency Medical Services Committee for Washington, D.C. and served as an instructor for the Washington D.C. Emergency Medical Systems Paramedic Training School. She also serves on the State of Maryland's Department of Health as a volunteer physician for Disaster Preparedness and Bioterrorism.

Dr. Cates has been a member of the American Medical Association since 1988 and became Board Certified by the American Board of Emergency Medicine in 1992. She is a Fellow in the American Academy of Emergency Medicine (FAAEM) as well as in the American College of Emergency Physicians (FACEP), and is a member of the National Medical Association. She is an elected member of the *National Register's Who's Who In Executives and Professionals*, and has been listed in the *2003 Guide to America's Top Physicians* by the Consumers' Research Council of America. Dr. Cates was awarded Oakwood College Alumna of the Year 2003 and raises funds for student scholarships. She is a lifetime member of the National Congress of Black Women as well as the Women Physicians Congress of the American Medical Association.

Dr. Cates has financially and spiritually supported students in their quest for higher education. She has also provided a place for fellowship and home-cooked meals to many students from Oakwood College and other schools, during their summer programs at Howard University.

Dr. Cates home schools their three children (Walesia II- age 8, Maurice II- age 6, and Maurcus- age 4) who have become dynamic, professional public speakers. They travel around the country with their parents, using their gift of oration to build up God's Kingdom of excellence in churches, schools, galas, concerts, various organizations, radio broadcasts and to public officials such as U.S. Senators, Congressmen and Diplomats. Dr. Cates co-produced a video chronicling selections of the children's live presentations entitled, *Words of Children, Volume One.*

In conjunction with the authorship of this book, she has founded the organization, Sisters C.A.R.E. (Sisters in Community Action Restoring Excellence) where Christian, professional women comfort, counsel, connect and celebrate women for the good of the community, the country, the church and the core family unit. Dr. Cates also hosts *In God's Image* family life conferences for churches, to mentor believers on *restoring the image of God in the family by restoring the image of God as family.*

Her vocal career is flourishing with the release of *My Cornerstone*, a debut CD. It contains anointed inspirational songs awesomely performed in Walesia's distinctive style. She is a songwriter as well. Her music is aired on Christian radio stations in the United States, Canada and Bermuda, as well as on 3ABN satellite television broadcast. She provides musical selections and concerts for local, regional, national and international audiences.

Dr. Cates is President and Medical Director of National CHECK UP, Inc., a community health education organization created to perpetuate the ideals of God's plan for physical, mental, emotional, financial and spiritual prosperity. In partnership with ministries that have mentored her, she supports outreach efforts in many countries of the world.

Despite her demanding schedule, she finds time to indulge in her leisure pursuit of maintaining a personally created arboretum, a floral garden paradise, which is enjoyed by many.

So you can see that Walesia Lynn Robinson Cates, M.D., FACEP, FAAEM, understands that she, as a woman, is indeed created in God's image and likeness and has received her own God-given dominion on planet earth. She is a motivated mother and a musical, medical, missionary ministering God's millennial message to multitudes in this post-modern age. She lives a life of employing hands, head and heart to bring pleasure to God and the message of health, happiness and hope to humankind. Walesia loves God. And Jesus Christ is her elder Brother.

Bibliography

Cairns, Earl E. *Christianity Through the Centuries.* Grand Rapids, MI: Zondervan,1996.

Cunningham, Loren and Hamilton, David Joel. *Why Not Women?* Seattle, Washington: YWAM Publishing, 2000.

Dake, Finis Jennings. *Dake's Annotated Reference Bible.* Lawrenceville, Georgia: Dake Publishing, 1963, 1991.

Holman Bible Dictionary and Concordance. Nashville, TN: Broadman & Holman Publishers, 1998.

Knight, George R. *Walking With Paul Through the Book of Romans.* Hagerstown, MD: Review and Herald Publishing Association, 2002.

Kohlenberger III, John R. *The Interlinear NIV Hebrew-English Old Testament.* Grand Rapids, MI: Zondervan Publishing House, 1987

Kroeger, Catherine Clark & Evans, Mary J. *The IVP Women's Bible Commentary.* Downers Grove, Ill.: InterVarsity Press, 2001.

Monroe, Miles. *Understanding the Purpose and Power of Woman.* New Kensington, PA: Whitaker House, 2001.

Nelson's A to Z Series. What Does the Bible Say About.... Nashville, TN: Thomas Nelson, Inc., 2001

New Strong's Expanded Exhaustive Concordance of the Bible. Nashville, TN: Thomas Nelson Publishers, 2001.

Stoddart, Errol T. *The Silent Shout.* Philadelphia, PA: Ecnerret Publishing Company, 2001

Scripture Index

Notes

Notes

Notes

Notes

Musician:

Published lyric soprano, performing since the age of 5 years.

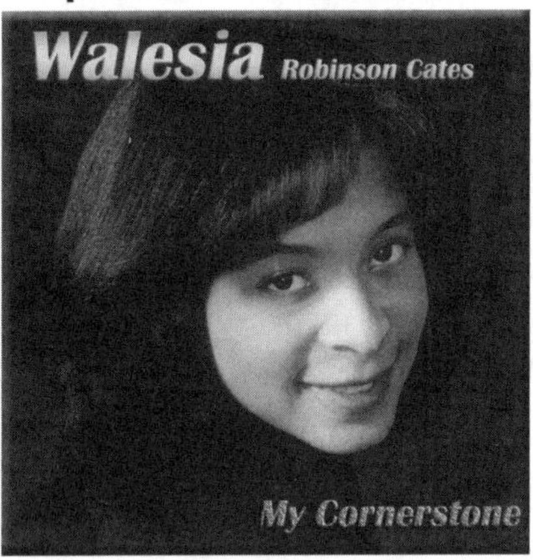

I have chosen the songs in this collection because of what they mean to me:

My Hope is Built on nothing less than Jesus' blood and His righteousness. All I have ever needed God has provided. That is why I can say, ***Great is Thy Faithfulness*** unto me. He's got the ***Whole World in His Hand***; and ***These are the Hands*** that bled for me. I can sing because I am so happy! Because I know without a doubt that ***His Eye is on the Sparrow***, and therefore is surely on me as well. And at the start of each new day, my Heavenly Father will ***Give Me Jesus*** anew for cleansing and covering. You see, Jesus is ***My Cornerstone***. He is the center and foundation of my life. He assures me through His Holy Spirit that ***It is Well With My Soul***. And on that great day, upon receiving the crown of ***Eternal Life***, I will shout with cries of joy how ***Jesus Led Me All the Way***.

To schedule a concert or to order products, please contact:

Wind, Word and Song Music
P.O. Box 703
Glenn Dale, Maryland 20769-2023
(800) 462-1422
wordandsong@catesco.org
www.catesco.org

Medical Doctor:

Board certified Emergency Medicine physician. Founder of an organization providing health education for communities nationwide.

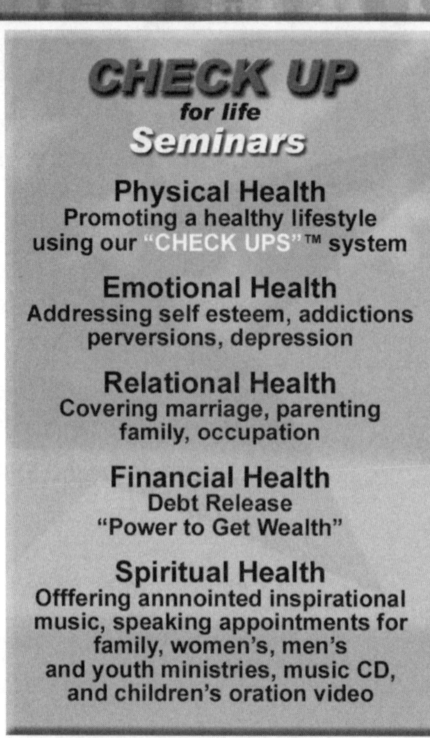

Mother:

Mother of three precious, home schooled children. She has developed an inspiring oration ministry with them called: "Cates Children Speak"

Available on Video:
"Words of Children Volume I"

For products and performances, please contact:

Dr. Walesia Cates Ministries
P.O. Box 703
Glenn Dale, Maryland 20769-2023
(800) 462-1422
drwalesiacates@catesco.org
www.catesco.org

Millennial Messenger:

Mentor to women. Through deposition of revelation knowledge from the Holy Spirit, backed by biblical research and historical record, she carries the message of hope to families everywhere that each family member has heavenly representation and "identity with Deity".

For speaking appointments, please contact:

Dr. Walesia Cates Ministries
P.O. Box 703
Glenn Dale, Maryland 20769-2023
1-800-462-1422
drwalesiacates@catesco.org
www.catesco.org

Motivator in the Community:

Founder of Sisters C.A.R.E., Inc. Created to comfort, counsel, connect and celebrate women for the good of the community, the country, the church, and the core family unit.

Sisters in Community Action Restoring Excellence

Counseling seminars on women's issues
Achievement support for academics and career
Rehabilitation seminars on addictions
Education seminars on health and personal finances

For information, seminar scheduling, and speaking appointments, please contact:

Dr. Walesia Robinson Cates
P.O. Box 703
Glenn Dale, MD 20769-2023
(800) 462-1422
sistersCARE@catesco.org
www.catesco.org

Mother Nature's Gardener

Accomplished gardener and horticulturist. Her arboretum is a natural, living sanctuary of peaceful beauty. Here, she walks with God in the cool of the day, as in the Garden of Eden.

For living color photographs, visit: www.catesco.org

Offering and Order Forms

☐ Yes! I understand this urgent need of restoration and unity in the family, in the community, in the church and society. I appreciate the gospel work you are doing and stand with you in prayer. I will tell others about this wonderful book.

☐ Yes! The gospel message must go into all the world. I would like to plant a seed of financial support to help this ministry reach families everywhere, so that the true image of God can be restored on earth in this generation.

Enclosed is my gift of:

☐ **$100** ☐ **$50** ☐ **$25** ☐ **$10** ☐ **$______**

Please place my gift on my credit card:

☐ VISA ☐ MasterCard ☐ DISCOVER ☐ AMERICAN EXPRESS

Name: ____

Address: ____

____

Card Number: ____________________________________

Expiration Date: _________________________________

Signature: ______________________________________

Phone: ____________________ Email: ____________________

☐ I have enclosed my gift of $25.00 dollars or more. Please send me "My Cornerstone" compact disc.

Thank you! May God bless you. Please make your checks payable to Dr. Walesia Cates Ministries. Mail or fax order form to P.O. Box 703, Glenn Dale, Maryland, 20769-2023. 1-800-462-1422 (toll free) 301-464-2003 (fax)

Gifts are tax deductible under IRS regulations.

For online ordering or donations, please visit www.catesco.org

You may write to me at **drwalesiacates@catesco.org**

Holy Spirit Mother $19.95

☐Yes! I would like to have my own copy or additional copies of this revolutionary book on family, marriage and gender relations from a biblical perspective, *Holy Spirit Mother.*

☐Yes! I would like to send a friend, pastor, group leader or family member a copy of this dynamic book, *Holy Spirit Mother.*

To purchase *Holy Spirit Mother,* please visit your local bookstore.
Or contact:
Catesco Press
1-800-276-8101 (toll free)
www.holyspiritmother.org (website and on-line store)
(301) 464-2003 (fax)
P.O. Box 703
Glenn Dale, MD 20769-2023

If purchasing by cashier's check or money order, please make payable to Dr. Walesia Cates Ministries.

Enclose $5.00 S&H for one book (plus $2 for each additional book), and mail or fax your name, address, zip code, telephone number and e-mail address.
For credit card purchases:

☐ VISA ☐ MasterCard ☐ DISCOVER ☐ AMERICAN EXPRESS

Name: ______________________________

Address: ______________________________

____

Card Number: ______________________________

Expiration Date: ______________________________

Signature: ______________________________

Phone: ______________ Email: ______________

Thank you! May God bless you.